Freedom's Battle

Being A Comprehensive Collection Of Writings And Speeches On The Present Situation

by

Mahatma Gandhi

Double9 BOOKS

FREEDOM'S BATTLE

BEING A COMPREHENSIVE COLLECTION OF WRITINGS AND SPEECHES ON THE PRESENT SITUATION

by Mahatma Gandhi

ISBN: 978-93-59321-91-2

Published by

DOUBLE 9 BOOKS
2/13-B, Ansari Road, Daryaganj
New Delhi - 110002
info@double9books.com
www.double9books.com
Tel. 011-40042856

ABOUT THE AUTHOR

Mohandas Karamchand Gandhi (October 2, 1869 - January 30, 1948) was an Indian lawyer, anti-colonial patriot, and political ethicist who led the successful movement for India's independence from British control through peaceful resistance. He sparked civil rights and freedom movements all across the world. The epithet Mahtm (from Sanskrit for 'great-souled, venerable') was initially ascribed to him in South Africa in 1914 and is now used worldwide. Gandhi, he was brought up in a Hindu family on the Gujarat coast, learned law at the Inner Temple in London, he was called to the bar at the age of 22 in June 1891. He traveled to South Africa in 1893 to represent an Indian merchant in a dispute after two uncertain years in India, when he was unable to establish a successful law practice. He afterwards spent 21 years in South Africa. It was here that Gandhi raised a family and first used nonviolent resistance in a civil rights struggle. In 1915, at the age of 45, he went to India and immediately began organizing peasants, farmers, and urban laborers to protest exorbitant land taxation and discrimination.

CONTENTS

I-INTRODUCTION

After the great war it is difficult, to point out a single nation that is happy; but this has come out of the war, that there is not a single nation outside India, that is not either free or striving to be free.

It is said that we, too, are on the road to freedom, that it is better to be on the certain though slow course of gradual unfoldment of freedom than to take the troubled and dangerous path of revolution whether peaceful or violent, and that the new Reforms are a half-way house to freedom.

The new constitution granted to India keeps all the military forces, both in the direction and in the financial control, entirely outside the scope of responsibility to the people of India. What does this mean? It means that the revenues of India are spent away on what the nation does not want. But after the mid-Eastern complications and the fresh Asiatic additions to British Imperial spheres of action. This Indian military servitude is a clear danger to national interests.

The new constitution gives no scope for retrenchment and therefore no scope for measures of social reform except by fresh taxation, the heavy burden of which on the poor will outweigh all the advantages of any reforms. It maintains all the existing foreign services, and the cost of the administrative machinery high as it already is, is further increased.

The reformed constitution keeps all the fundamental liberties of person, property, press, and association completely under bureaucratic control. All those laws which give to the irresponsible officers of the Executive Government of India absolute powers to override the popular will, are still unrepealed. In spite of the tragic price paid in the Punjab for demonstrating the danger of unrestrained power in the hands of a foreign bureaucracy and the inhumanity of spirit by which tyranny in a panic will seek to save itself, we stand just where we were before, at the mercy of the Executive in respect of all our fundamental liberties.

Not only is Despotism intact in the Law, but unparalleled crimes and cruelties against the people have been encouraged and even after boastful admissions and clearest proofs, left unpunished. The spirit of unrepentant cruelty has thus been allowed to permeate the whole administration.

THE MUSSALMAN AGONY

To understand our present condition it is not enough to realise the general political servitude. We should add to it the reality and the extent of the injury inflicted by Britain on Islam, and thereby on the Mussalmans of India. The articles of Islamic faith which it is necessary to understand in order to realise why Mussalman India, which was once so loyal is now so strongly moved to the contrary are easily set out and understood. Every religion should be interpreted by the professors of that religion. The sentiments and religious ideas of Muslims founded on the traditions of long generations cannot be altered now by logic or cosmopolitanism, as others understand it. Such an attempt is the more unreasonable when it is made not even as a bonafide and independent effort of proselytising logic or reason, but only to justify a treaty entered into for political and worldly purposes.

The Khalifa is the authority that is entrusted with the duty of defending Islam. He is the successor to Muhammad and the agent of God on earth. According to Islamic tradition he must possess sufficient temporal power effectively to protect Islam against non-Islamic powers and he should be one elected or accepted by the Mussalman world.

The Jazirat-ul-Arab is the area bounded by the Red Sea, the Arabian Sea, the Persian Gulf, and the waters of the Tigris and the Euphrates. It is the sacred Home of Islam and the centre towards which Islam throughout the world turns in prayer. According to the religious injunctions of the Mussalmans, this entire area should always be under Muslim control, its scientific border being believed to be a protection for the integrity of Islamic life and faith. Every Mussalman throughout the world is enjoined to sacrifice his all, if necessary, for preserving the Jazirat-ul-Arab under complete Muslim control.

The sacred places of Islam should be in the possession of the Khalifa. They should not merely be free for the entry of the Mussalmans of the world by the grace or the license of non-Muslim powers, but should be the possession and property of Islam in the fullest degree.

It is a religions obligation, on every Mussalman to go forth and help the Khalifa in every possible way where his unaided efforts in the defence of the Khilifat have failed.

The grievance of the Indian Mussalmans is that a government that pretends to protect and spread peace and happiness among them has no right to ignore or set aside these articles of their cherished faith.

According to the Peace Treaty imposed on the nominal Government at Constantinople, the Khalifa far from having the temporal authority or power needed to protect Islam, is a prisoner in his own city. He is to have no real fighting force, army or navy, and the financial control over his own territories is vested in other Governments. His capital is cut off from the rest of his possessions by an intervening permanent military occupation. It is needless to say that under these conditions he is absolutely incapable of protecting Islam as the Mussulmans of the world understand it.

The Jazirat-ul-Arab is split up; a great part of it given to powerful non-Muslim Powers, the remnant left with petty chiefs dominated all round by non-Muslim Governments.

The Holy places of Islam are all taken out of the Khalifa's kingdom, some left in the possession of minor Muslim chiefs of Arabia entirely dependent on European control, and some relegated to newly-formed non-Muslim states.

In a word, the Mussalman's free choice of a Khalifa such as Islamic tradition defines is made an unreality.

THE HINDU DHARMA

The age of misunderstanding and mutual warfare among religions is gone. If India has a mission of its own to the world, it is to establish the unity and the truth of all religions. This unity is established by mutual help and understanding between the various religions. It has come as a rare privilege to the Hindus in the fulfilment of this mission of India to stand up in defence of Islam against the onslaught of the earth-greed of the military powers of the west.

The Dharma of Hinduism in this respect is placed beyond all doubt by the Bhagavat Gita.

Those who are the votaries of other Gods and worship them with faith--even they, O Kaunteya, worship me alone, though not as the Shastra requires--IX, 23.

Whoever being devoted wishes in perfect faith to worship a particular form, of such a one I maintain the same faith unshaken,--VII 21.

Hinduism will realise its fullest beauty when in the fulfilment of this cardinal tenet, its followers offer themselves as sacrifice for the protection of the faith of their brothers, the Mussalmans.

If Hindus and Mussalmans attain the height of courage and sacrifice that is needed for this battle on behalf of Islam against the greed of the West, a victory will be won not alone for Islam, but for Christianity itself. Militarism has robbed the crucified God of his name and his very cross and the World has been mistaking it to be Christianity. After the battle of Islam is won, Islam and Hinduism together can emancipate Christianity itself from the lust for power and wealth which have strangled it now and the true Christianity of the Gospels will be established. This battle of non-cooperation with its suffering and peaceful withdrawal of service will once for all establish its superiority over the power of brute force and unlimited slaughter.

What a glorious privilege it is to play our part in this history of the world, when Hinduism and Christianity will unite on behalf of Islam, and in that strife of mutual love and support each religion will attain its own truest shape and beauty.

AN ENDURING TREATY

Swaraj for India has two great problems, one internal and the other external. How can Hindus and Mussalmans so different from each other form a strong and united nation governing themselves peacefully? This was the question for years, and no one could believe that the two communities could suffer for each other till the miracle was actually worked. The Khilafat has solved the problem. By the magic of suffering, each has truly touched and captured the other's heart, and the Nation now is strong and united.

Not internal strength and unity alone has the Khilafat brought to India. The great block in the way of Indian aspiration for full freedom was the problem of external defence. How is India, left to herself defend her frontiers against her Mussalman neighbours? None but emasculated nations would accept such difficulties and responsibilities as an answer to the demand for freedom. It is only a people whose mentality has been perverted that can soothe itself with the domination by one race from a distant country, as a preventative against the aggression of another, a permanent and natural neighbour. Instead of developing strength to protect ourselves against those near whom we are permanently placed, a feeling of incurable impotence has been generated. Two strong and brave nations can live side by side, strengthening each other through enforcing constant vigilance, and maintain in full vigour each its own national strength, unity, patriotism and resources. If a nation wishes to be respected by its neighbours it has to develop and enter into honourable treaties. These are the only natural conditions of national liberty; but not a surrender to distant military powers to save oneself from one's neighbours.

The Khilafat has solved the problem of distrust of Asiatic neighbours out of our future. The Indian struggle for the freedom of Islam has brought about a more lasting *entente* and a more binding treaty between the people of India and the people of the Mussalman states around it than all the ententes and treaties among the Governments of Europe. No wars of aggression are possible where the common people on the two sides have become grateful friends. The faith of the Mussulman is a better sanction than the seal of the European Diplomats and plenipotentiaries. Not only has this great friendship between India and the Mussulman States around it removed for all time the fear of Mussulman aggression from outside, but it has erected round India, a solid wall of defence against all aggression from beyond against all greed from Europe, Russia or elsewhere. No secret diplomacy could establish a better *entente* or a stronger federation than what this open and non-governmental treaty between Islam and India has established. The Indian support of the Khilafat has, as if by a magic wand, converted what Was once the Pan-Islamic terror for Europe into a solid wall of friendship and defence for India.

THE BRITISH CONNECTION

Every nation like every individual is born free. Absolute freedom is the birthright of every people. The only limitations are those which a people may place over themselves. The British connection is invaluable as long as it is a defence against any worse connection sought to be imposed by violence. But it is only a means to an end, not a mandate of Providence of Nature. The alliance of neighbours, born of suffering for each other's sake, for ends that purify those that suffer, is necessarily a more natural and more enduring bond than one that has resulted from pure greed on the one side and weakness on the other. Where such a natural and enduring alliance has been accomplished among Asiatic peoples and not only between the respective governments, it may truly be felt to be more valuable than the British connection itself, after that connection has denied freedom or equality, and even justice.

THE ALTERNATIVE

Is violence or total surrender the only choice open to any people to whom Freedom or Justice is denied? Violence at a time when the whole world has learnt from bitter experience the futility of violence is unworthy of a country whose ancient people's privilege, it was, to see this truth long ago.

Violence may rid a nation of its foreign masters but will only enslave it from inside. No nation can really be free which is at the mercy of its army and its military heroes. If a people rely for freedom on its soldiers, the soldiers will rule the country, not the people. Till the recent awakening of the workers of Europe, this was the only freedom which the powers of Europe really enjoyed. True freedom can exist only when those who produce, not those who destroy or know only to live on other's labour, are the masters.

Even were violence the true road to freedom, is violence possible to a nation which has been emasculated and deprived of all weapons, and the whole world is hopelessly in advance of all our possibilities in the manufacture and the wielding of weapons of destruction.

Submission or withdrawal of co-operation is the real and only alternative before India. Submission to injustice puts on the tempting garb of peace and, gradual progress, but there is no surer way to death than submission to wrong.

THE FIFTH UPAYA

Our ancients classified the arts of conquest into four well-known

Upayas

. Sama, Dana, Uheda, and Danda. A fifth Upuya was recognised sometimes by our ancients, which they called

Upeshka

. It is this

Punchamopaya

that is placed by Mahatma Gandhi before the people of India in the form of Non-cooperation as an alternative, besides violence, to surrender.

Where in any case negotiations have failed and the enemy is neither corruptible nor incapable of being divided, and a resort to violence has failed or would certainly be futile the method of *Upeshka* remains to be applied to the case. Indeed, when the very existence of the power we seek to defeat really depends on our continuous co-operation with it, and where our *Upeskha* its very life, our *Upeskha* or non-co-operation is the most natural and most effective expedient that we can employ to bend it to our will.

No Englishman believes that his nation can rule or keep India for a day unless the people of India actively co-operate to maintain that rule. Whether the co-operation be given willingly or through ignorance, cupidity, habit or fear, the withdrawal of that co-operation means impossibility of foreign rule in India. Some of us may not realise this, but those who govern us have long ago known and are now keenly alive to this truth. The active assistance of the people of this country in the supply of the money, men, and knowledge of the languages, customs and laws of the land, is the main-spring of the continuous life of the foreign administration. Indeed the circumstances of British rule in this country are such that but for a double supply of co-operation on the part of the governed, it must have broken down long ago. Any system of race domination is unnatural, and can be kept up only by active coercion through a foreign-recruited public, service invested with large powers, however much it may be helped by the perversion of mentality shaping the education of the youth of the country. The foreign recruited service must necessarily be very highly paid. This creates a wrong standard for the Indian recruited officials also. Military expenditure has to cover not only the needs of defence against foreign aggression, but also the possibilities of internal unrest and rebellion. Police charges have to go beyond the prevention and deletion of ordinary crime, for though this would be the only expenditure over the police of a self-governing people where any nation governs anther, a large chapter of artificial crime has to be added to the penal code, and the work of the police extended accordingly. The military and public organisations must also be such as not only to result in outside efficiency, but also at the same time guarantee internal impotency. This is to be achieved by the adjustment and careful admixture of officers and units from different races. All this can be and is maintained only by extra cost and extra-active co-operation on the part of the people. The slightest withdrawal of assistance must put such machinery out of gear. This is the basis of the programme of progressive non violent non-co-operation that has been adopted by the National Congress.

SOME OBJECTIONS

The powerful character of the measure, however, leads some to object to non-co-operation because of that very reason. Striking as it does at the very root of Government in India, they fear that non-co-operation must lead to anarchy, and that the remedy is worse than the disease. This is an objection arising out of insufficient allowance for human nature. It is assumed that the British people will allow their connection with India to cease rather than remedy the wrongs for which we seek justice. If this assumption be correct, no doubt it must lead to separation and possibly also anarchy for a time. If the operatives in a factory have grievances, negotiations having failed, a strike would on a similar argument be never admissible. Unyielding obstinacy being presumed, it must end in the closing down of the factory and break up of the men. But if in ninety-nine out of a hundred cases it is not the case that strikes end in this manner, it is more unlikely that, instead of righting the manifest wrongs that India complains about, the British people will value their Indian Dominion so low as to prefer to allow us to non-co-operate up to the point of separation. It would be a totally false reading of British character and British history. But if such wicked obstinacy be ultimately shown by a government, far be it from us to prefer peace at the price of abject surrender to wrong. There is no anarchy greater than the moral anarchy of surrender to unrepentant wrong. We may, however, be certain that if we show the strength and unity necessary for non-co-operation, long before we progress with it far, we shall have developed true order and true self-government wherein there is no place for anarchy.

Another fear sometimes expressed that, if non-co-operation were to succeed, the British would have to go, leaving us unable to defend ourselves against foreign aggression. If we have the self-respect, the patriotism, the tenacious purpose, and the power of organisation that are necessary to drive the British out from their entrenched position, no lesser foreign power will dare after that, undertake the futile task of conquering or enslaving us.

It is sometimes said that non-co-operation is negative and destructive of the advantages which a stable government has conferred on us. That non-co-operation is negative is merely a half-truth. Non-co-operation with the government means greater co-operation among ourselves, greater mutual dependence among the many different castes and classes of our country. Non-co-operation is not mere negation. It will lead to the recovery of the lost art of co-operation among ourselves. Long dependence on an outside government which by its interference suppressed or prevented the consequences of our differences has made us forget the duty of mutual trust and the art of friendly adjustment. Having allowed Government to do everything for us, we have gradually become incapable of doing anything for ourselves. Even if we had no grievance against this Government, non-co-operation with it for a time would be desirable so far as it would perforce lead us to trusting and working with one another and thereby strengthen the bonds of national unity.

The most tragic consequence of dependence on the complex machinery of a foreign government is the atrophy of the communal sense. The direct touch with administrative cause and effect is lost. An outside protector performs all the necessary functions of the community in a mysterious manner, and communal duties are not realised by the people. The one reason addressed by those who deny to us the capacity for self-rule is the insufficient appreciation by the people of communal duties and discipline. It is only by actually refraining for a time from dependence on Government that we can regain self-reliance, learn first-hand the value of communal duties and build up true national co-operation. Non-co-operation is a practical and positive training in Swadharma, and Swadharma alone can lead up to Swaraj.

The negative is the best and most impressive method of enforcing the value of the positive. Few outside government circles realise in the present police anything but tyranny and corruption. But if the units of the present police were withdrawn we would soon perforce set about organising a substitute, and most people would realise the true social value of a police force. Few realise in the present taxes anything but coercion and waste, but most people would soon see that a share of every man's income is due for common purposes and that there are many limitations to the economical management of public institutions; we would begin once again to contribute directly, build up and maintain national institutions in the place of those that now mysteriously spring up and live under Government orders.

EMANCIPATION

Freedom is a priceless thing. But it is a stable possession only when it is acquired by a nation's strenuous effort. What is not by chance or outward circumstance, or given by the generous impulse of a tyrant prince or people is not a reality. A nation will truly enjoy freedom only when in the process of winning or defending its freedom, it has been purified and consolidated through and through, until liberty has become a part of its very soul. Otherwise it would be but a change of the form of government, which might please the fancy of politicians, or satisfy the classes in power, but could never emancipate a people. An Act of Parliament can never create citizens in Hindustan. The strength, spirit, and happiness of a people who have fought and won their liberty cannot be got by Reform Acts. Effort and sacrifice are the necessary conditions of real stable emancipation. Liberty unacquired, merely found, will on the test fail like the Dead-Sea-apple or the magician's plenty.

The war that the people of India have declared and which will purify and consolidate India, and forge for her a true and stable liberty is a war with the latest and most effective weapon. In this war, what has hitherto been in the world an undesirable but necessary incident in freedom's battles, the killing of innocent men, has been eliminated; and that which is the true essential for forging liberty, the self-purification and self-strengthening of men and women has been kept pure and unalloyed. It is for men, women and youth, every one of them that lives in and loves India, to do his bit in this battle, not waiting for others, not calculating the chances of his surviving the battle to enjoy the fruits of his sacrifice. Soldiers in the old-world wars did not insure their lives before going to the front. The privilege of youth in special is for country's sake to exercise their comparative freedom and give up the yearning for lives and careers built on the slavery of the people.

That on which a foreign government truly rests whatever may be the illusions on their or our part is not the strength of its armed forces, but our own co-operation. Actual service on the part of one generation, and educational preparation for future service on the part of the next generation are the two main branches of this co-operation of slaves in the perpetuation of slavery. The boycott of government service and the law-courts is aimed at the first, the boycott of government controlled schools is to stop the second. If either the one or the other of these two branches of co-operation is withdrawn in sufficient measure, there will be an automatic and perfectly peaceful change from slavery to liberty.

The beat preparation for any one who desires to take part in the great battle now going on is a silent study of the writings and speeches collected herein, and proposed to be completed in a supplementary volume to be soon issued.

C. RAJAGOPALACHAR

II-THE KHILAFAT

WHY I HAVE JOINED THE KHILAFAT MOVEMENT

An esteemed South African friend who is at present living in England has written to me a letter from which I make the following excerpts:--

> "You will doubtless remember having met me in South Africa at the time when the Rev. J.J. Doke was assisting you in your campaign there and I subsequently returned to England deeply impressed with the rightness of your attitude in that country. During the months before war I wrote and lectured and spoke on your behalf in several places which I do not regret. Since returning from military service, however, I have noticed from the papers that you appear to be adopting a more militant attitude... I notice a report in "The Times" that you are assisting and countenancing a union between the Hindus and Moslems with a view of embarrassing England and the Allied Powers in the matter of the dismemberment of the Ottoman Empire or the ejection of the Turkish Government from Constantinople. Knowing as I do your sense of justice and your humane instincts I feel that I am entitled, in view of the humble part that I have taken to promote your interests on this side, to ask you whether this latter report is correct. I cannot believe that you have wrongly countenanced a movement to place the cruel and unjust despotism of the Stamboul Government above the interests of humanity, for if any country has crippled these interests in the East it has surely been Turkey. I am personally familiar with the conditions in Syria and Armenia and I can only suppose that if the report, which "The Times" has published is correct, you have thrown to one side, your moral responsibilities and allied yourself with one of the prevailing anarchies. However, until I hear that this is not your attitude I cannot prejudice my mind. Perhaps you will do me the favour of sending me a reply."

I have sent a reply to the writer. But as the views expressed in the quotation are likely to be shared by many of my English friends and as I do not wish, if I can possibly help it, to forfeit their friendship or their esteem I shall endeavour to state my position as clearly as I can on the Khilafat question. The letter shows what risk public men run through irresponsible journalism. I have not seen

The Times

report, referred to by my friend. But it is evident that the report has made the writer to suspect my alliance with "the prevailing anarchies" and to think that I have "thrown to one side" my "moral responsibilities."

It is just my sense of moral responsibilities which has made me take up the Khilafat question and to identify myself entirely with the Mahomedans. It is perfectly true that I am assisting and countenancing the union between Hindus and Muslims, but certainly not with "a view of embarrassing England and the Allied Powers in the matter of the dismemberment of the Ottoman Empire," it is contrary to my creed to embarrass governments or anybody else. This does not how ever mean that certain acts of mine may not result in embarrassment. But I should not hold myself responsible for having caused embarrassment when I resist the wrong of a wrong-doer by refusing assistance in his wrong-doing. On the Khilafat question I refuse to be party to a broken pledge. Mr. Lloyd George's solemn declaration is practically the whole of the case for Indian Mahomedans and when that case is fortified by scriptural authority it becomes unanswerable. Moreover, it is incorrect to say that I have "allied myself to one of the prevailing anarchies" or that I have wrongly countenanced the movement to place the cruel and unjust despotism of the Stamboul Government above the interests of humanity. In the whole of the Mahomedan demand there is no insistance on the retention of the so-called unjust despotism of the Stamboul Government; on the contrary the Mahomedans have accepted the principle of taking full guarantees from that Government for the protection of non-Muslim minorities. I do not know how far the condition of Armenia and Syria may be considered an 'anarchy' and how far the Turkish Government may be held responsible for it. I much suspect that the reports from these quarters are much exaggerated and that the European powers are themselves in a measure responsible for what misrule there may be in Armenia and Syria. But I am in no way interested in supporting Turkish or any other anarchy. The Allied Powers can easily prevent it by means other than that of ending Turkish rule or dismembering and weakening the Ottoman Empire. The Allied Powers are not dealing with a new situation. If Turkey was to be partitioned, the position should have been made clear at the commencement of the war. There would then have been no question of a broken pledge. As it is, no Indian Mahomedan has any regard for the promises of British Ministers. In his opinion, the cry against Turkey is that of Christianity *vs.* Islam with England as the louder in the cry. The latest cablegram from Mr. Mahomed Ali strengthens the impression, for he says that unlike as in England his deputation is receiving much support from the French Government and the people.

Thus, if it is true, as I hold it is true that the Indian Mussalmans have a cause that is just and is supported by scriptural authority, then for the Hindus not to support them to the utmost would be a cowardly breach of brotherhood and they would forfeit all claim to consideration from their Mahomedan countrymen. As a public-server therefore, I would be unworthy of the position I claim, if I did not support Indian Mussalmans in their struggle to maintain the Khilafat in accordance with their religious belief. I believe that in supporting them I am rendering a service to the Empire, because by assisting my Mahomedan countrymen to give a disciplined expression to their sentiment it becomes possible to make the agitation thoroughly, orderly and even successful.

THE TURKISH TREATY

The Turkish treaty will be out on the 10th of May. It is stated to provide for the internationalisation of the Straits, the occupation of Gallipoli by the Allies, the maintenance of Allied contingents in Constantinople and the appointment of a Commission of Control over Turkish finances. The San Remo Conference has entrusted Britain with Mandates for Mesopotamia and Palestine and France with the Mandate for Syria. As regards Smyrna the accounts so far received inform that Turkish suzerainty over Smyrna will be indicated by the fact that the population will not be entitled to send delegates to the Greek Parliament but at the end of five years local Smyrna Parliament will have the right of voting in favour of union with Greece and in such an event Turkish suzerainty will cease. Turkish suzerainty will be confined to the area within the Chatalja lines. With regard to Emir Foisul's position there is no news except that the Mandates of Britain and France transform his military title into a civil title.

*   *   *   *   *

We have given above the terms of the Turkish treaty as indicated in Router's messages. These reports are incomplete and all of them are not equally authenticated. But if these terms are true, they are a challenge to the Muslim demands. Turkish Sovereignty is confined to the Chatalja lines. This means that the Big Three of the Supreme Council have cut off Thrace from Turkish dominions. This is a distinct breach of the pledge given by one of these Three, *viz.*, the Premier of the British Empire. To remain within the Chatalja lines and, we are afraid, as a dependent of the Allies, is for the Sultan a humiliating position inconsistent with the Koranic injunctions. Such a restricted position of the Turks is virtually a success of the bag and baggage school.

It is not yet known how the Supreme Council disposed of the rich and renowned lands of Asia Minor. If Mr. Lloyd George's views recently expressed in this respect have received the Allies' sanction--it is probable--nothing less than a common control is expected. The decision in the case of Smyrna will be satisfying to none, though the Allies seem to have made by their arrangement a skillful attempt to please all the parties concerned. Mr. Lloyd George, in his reply to the Khilafat Deputation, had talked about the careful investigations by an impartial committee and had added; "The great majority of the population undoubtedly prefer Greek rule to Turkish rule, so I understand" But the decision postpones to carry out his understanding till a period of five years.

* * * * *

When we come to the question of mandates, the Allied Powers' motives come out more distinctly. The Arabs' claim of independence was used as a difficulty against keeping Turkish Sovereignty. This was defended in the of self-determination and by pointing out parallels of Transylvania and other provinces. When the final moment came, the Allies have ventured to divide the spoils amongst themselves. Britain is given the mandate over Mesopotamia and Palestine and France has the mandate over Syria. The Arab delegation complains in their note lately issued expressing their disappointment at the Supreme Council's decision with regard to the Arab liberated countries, which, it declares, is contrary to the principle of self-determination.

So what little news has arrived about the Turkish treaty, is uniformly disquieting. The Moslems have found sufficient ground to honour Russia, more than the Allies. Russia has recognised the freedom of Khiva and Bokhara. The Moslem world, as H. M. the Amir of Afghanistan said in his speech, will feel grateful towards Russia in spite of all the rumours abroad about its anarchy and disorder, whereas the whole Moslem world will resent the action of the other European nations who have allied with each other to carry out a joint coercion and extinction of Turkey in the name of self-determination and partly in the guise of the interest of civilization.

The terms of the Turkish treaty are not only a breach of the Premier's pledge, not only a sin against the principle of self-determination, but they also show a reckless indifference of the Allied Powers towards the Koranic injunctions. The terms point out that Mr. Lloyd George's misinformed ideas of Khilafat have prevailed in the Council. Like Mr. Lloyd George other statesmen also at San Remo have compared Caliphate with Popedom and ignored the Koronic idea of associating spiritual power with temporal power. These misguided statesmen were too much possessed by haughtiness and so they refused to receive any enlightenment on the question of Khilafat from the Deputation. They could have corrected themselves had they heard Mr. Mahomed Ali on this point. Speaking at the Essex Hall meeting Mr. Mahomed Ali distinguished between Popedom and Caliphate and clearly explained what Caliphate means. He said:

> "Islam is supernational and not national, the basis of Islamic sympathy is a common outlook on life and common culture.... And it has two centres. The personal centre is the island of Arabia. The Khalifa is the Commander of the Faithful and his orders must be obeyed by all Muslims so long and so long only, as they are not at variance with the Commandments of God and the Traditions of the Prophet. But since there is no lacerating distinction between things temporal and things spiritual, the Khalifa is something more than a Pope and cannot be "Vaticanised." But he is also less than a Pope for he is not infallible. If he persists in un-Islamic conduct we can depose him. And we have deposed him more than once. But so long as he orders only that which Islam demands we must support him. He and no other ruler is the Defender of *our* faith."

These few words could have removed the mis-undertakings rooted in the minds of those that at San Remo, if they were in earnest for a just solution. But Mr. Mahomed Ali's deputation was not given any hearing by the Peace Conference. They were told that the Peace Conference had already heard the official delegation of India on this question. But the wrong notions the Allies still entertain about Caliphate are a sufficient indication of the effects of the work of this official delegation. The result of these wrong notions is the present settlement and this unjust settlement will unsettle the world. They know not what they do.

TURKISH PEACE TERMS

The question of question to-day is the Khilafat question, otherwise known as that of the Turkish peace terms. His Excellency the Viceroy deserves our thanks for receiving the joint deputation even at this late hour, especially when he was busy preparing to receive the head of the different provinces. His Excellency must be thanked for the unfailing courtesy with which he received the deputation and the courteous language in which his reply was couched. But mere courtesy, valuable as it is at all times, never so valuable as at this, is not enough at this critical moment. 'Sweet words butter no parsnips' is a proverb more applicable to-day than ever before. Behind the courtesy there was the determination to punish Turkey. Punishment of Turkey is a thing which Muslim sentiment cannot tolerate for a moment.

Muslim soldiers are as responsible for the result of the war as any others. It was to appease them that Mr. Asquith said when Turkey decided to join the Central Powers that the British Government had no designs on Turkey and that His Majesty's Government would never think of punishing the Sultan for the misdeeds of the Turkish Committee. Examined by that standard the Viceregal reply is not only disappointing but it is a fall from truth and justice.

What is this British Empire? It is as much Mahomedan and Hindu as it is Christian. Its religious neutrality is not a virtue, or if it is, it is a virtue of necessity. Such a mighty Empire could not be held together on any other terms. British ministers are therefore bound to protect Mahomedan interests as any other. Indeed as the Muslim rejoinder says, they are bound to make the cause their own. What is the use of His Excellency having presented the Muslim claim before the Conference? If the cause is lost the Mahomedans will be entitled to think that Britain did not do her duty by them. And the Viceregal reply confirms the view. When His Excellency says that Turkey must suffer for her having joined the Central Powers he but expresses the opinion of British ministers. We hope, therefore, with the framers of the Muslim rejoinder that His Majesty's ministers will mend the mistakes if any have been committed and secure a settlement that would satisfy Mahomedan sentiment.

What does the sentiment demand? The preservation of the Khilafat with such guarantee as may be necessary for the protection of the interests of the non-Muslim races living under Turkish rule and the Khalif's control over Arabia and the Holy Places with such arrangement as may be required for guaranteeing Arab self-rule, should the Arabs desire it. It is hardly possible to state the claim more fairly than has been done. It is a claim backed by justice, by the declarations of British ministers and by the unanimous Hindu and Muslim opinion. It would be midsummer madness to reject or whittle down a claim so backed.

THE SUZERAINTY OVER ARABIA

> "As I told you in my last letter I think Mr. Gandhi has made a serious mistake in the Kailafat business. The Indian Mahomedans base their demand on the assertion that their religion requires the Turkish rule over Arabia: but when they have against them in this matter, the Arabs themselves, it is impossible to regard the theory of the Indian Mahomedans as essential to Islam. After all if the Arabs do not represent Islam, who does? It is as if the German Roman Catholics made a demand in the name of Roman Catholicism with Rome and the Italians making a contrary demand. But even if the religion of the Indian Mahomedans did require that Turkish rule should

be imposed upon the Arabs against their will, one could not, now-a-days, recognise as a really religious demand, one which required the continued oppression of one people by another. When an assurance was given at the beginning of the war to the Indian Mahomedans that the Mahomedan religion would be respected, that could never have meant that a temporal sovereignty which violated the principles of self-determination would be upheld. We could not now stand by and see the Turks re-conquer the Arabs (for the Arabs would certainly fight against them) without grossly betraying the Arabs to whom we have given pledges. It is not true that the Arab hostility to the Turks was due simply to European suggestion. No doubt, during the war we availed ourselves of the Arab hostility to the Turks to get another ally, but the hostility had existed long before the war. The Non-Turkish Mahomedan subjects of the Sultan in general wanted to get rid of his rule. It is the Indian Mahomedans who have no experience of that rule who want to impose it on others. As a matter of fact the idea of any restoration of Turkish rule in Syria or Arabia, seems so remote from all possibilities that to discuss it seems like discussing a restoration of the Holy Roman Empire. I cannot conceive what series of events could bring it about. The Indian Mahomedans certainly could not march into Arabia themselves and conquer the Arabs for the Sultan. And no amount of agitation and trouble in India would ever induce England to put back Turkish rule in Arabia. In this matter it is not English Imperialism which the Indian Mahomedans are up against, but the mass of English Liberal and Humanitarian opinion, the mass of the better opinion of England, which wants self-determination to go forward in India. Supposing the Indian Mahomedans could stir up an agitation so violent in India as to sever the connection between India and the British Crown, still they would not be any nearer to their purpose. For to-day they do have considerable influence on British world-policy. Even if in this matter of the Turkish question their influence has not been sufficient to turn the scale against the very heavy weights on the other side, it has weighed in the scale. But apart from the British connection, Indian Mahomedans would have no influence at all outside India. They would not count for more in world politics than the Mahomedans of China. I think it is likely (apart from the pressure of America on the other side. I should say certain) that the influence of the Indian Mahomedans may at any rate avail to keep the Sultan in Constantinople. But I doubt whether they will gain any advantage by doing so. For a Turkey cut down to the Turkish parts of Asia-Minor, Constantinople would be a very inconvenient capital. I think its inconvenience would more than outweigh the sentimental gratification of keeping up a phantom of the old Ottoman Empire. But if the

> Indian Mahomedans want the Sultan to retain his place in Constantinople I think the assurances given officially by the Viceroy in India now binds us to insist on his remaining there and I think he will remain there in spite of America."

This is an extract, from the letter of an Englishman enjoying a position in Great Britain, to a friend in India. It is a typical letter, sober, honest, to the point and put in such graceful language that whilst it challenges you, it commands your respect by its very gracefulness. But it is just this attitude based upon insufficient or false information which has ruined many a cause in the British Isles. The superficiality, the one-sidedness the inaccuracy and often even dishonesty that have crept into modern journalism, continuously mislead honest men who want to see nothing but justice done. Then there are always interested groups whose business it is to serve their ends by means of faul or food. And the honest Englishman wishing to vote for justice but swayed by conflicting opinions and dominated by distorted versions, often ends by becoming an instrument of injustice.

The writer of the letter quoted above has built up convincing argument on imaginary data. He has successfully shown that the Mahomedan case, as it has been presented to him, is a rotten case. In India, where it is not quite easy to distort facts about the Khilafat, English friends admit the utter justice of the Indian-Mahomedan claim. But they plead helplessness and tell us that the Government of India and Mr. Montagu have done all it was humanly possible for them to do. And if now the judgment goes against Islam, Indian Mahomedans should resign themselves to it. This extraordinary state of things would not be possible except under this modern rush and preoccupations of all responsible people.

Let us for a moment examine the case as it has been imagined by the writer. He suggests that Indian Mahomedans want Turkish rule in Arabia in spite of the opposition of the Arabs themselves, and that, if the Arabs do not want Turkish rule, the writer argues, no false religions sentiment can be permitted to interfere with self-determination of the Arabs when India herself has been pleading for that very status. Now the fact is that the Mahomedans, as is known to everybody who has at all studied the case, have never asked for Turkish rule in Arabia in opposition to the Arabs. On the contrary, they have said that they have no intention of resisting Arabian self-government. All they ask for is Turkish suzerainty over Arabia which would guarantee complete self-rule for the Arabs. They want Khalif's control of the Holy Places of Islam. In other words they ask for nothing more than what was guaranteed by Mr. Lloyd George and on the strength of which guarantee Mahomedan soldiers split their blood on behalf of the Allied Powers. All the elaborate argument therefore and the cogent reasoning of the above extract fall to pieces based as they are upon a case that has never existed. I have thrown myself heart and soul into this question because British pledges abstract justice, and religious sentiment coincide. I can conceive the possibility of a blind and fanatical religious sentiment existing in opposition to pure justice. I should then resist the former and fight for the latter. Nor would I insist upon pledges given dishonestly to support an unjust cause as has happened with England in the case of the secret treaties. Resistance there becomes not only lawful but obligatory on the part of a nation that prides itself on its righteousness.

It is unnecessary for me to examine the position imagined by the English friend, viz., how India would have fared had she been an independent power. It is unnecessary because Indian Mahomedans, and for that matter India, are fighting for a cause that is admittedly just; a cause in aid of which they are invoking the whole-hearted support of the British people. I would however venture to suggest that this is a cause in which mere sympathy will not suffice. It is a cause which demands support that is strong enough to bring about substantial justice.

FURTHER QUESTIONS ANSWERED

I have been overwhelmed with public criticism and private advice and even anonymous letters telling me exactly what I should do. Some are impatient that I do not advise immediate and extensive non-co-operation; others tell me what harm I am doing the country by throwing it knowingly in a tempest of violence on either side. It is difficult for me to deal with the whole of the criticism, but I would summarize some of the objections and endeavour to answer them to the best of my ability. These are in addition to those I have already answered:--

(1) Turkish claim is immoral or unjust and how can I, a lover of truth and justice, support it? (2) Even if the claim be just in theory, the Turk is hopelessly incapable, weak and cruel. He does not deserve any assistance.

(3) Even if Turkey deserves all that is claimed for her, why should I land India in an international struggle?

(4) It is no part of the Indian Mahomedans' business to meddle in this affair. If they cherish any political ambition, they have tried, they have failed and they should now sit still. If it is a religious matter with them, it cannot appeal to the Hindu reason in the manner it is put and in any case Hindus ought not to identify themselves with Mahomedans in their religious quarrel with Christendom.

(5) In no case should I advocate non-co-operation which in its extreme sense is nothing but a rebellion, no matter how peaceful it may be.

(6) Moreover, my experience of last year must show me that it is beyond the capacity of any single human being to control the forces of violence that are lying dormant in the land.

(7) Non-co-operation is futile because people will never respond in right earnest, and reaction that might afterwards set in will be worse than the state of hopefulness we are now in.

(8) Non-co-operation will bring about cessation of all other activities, even working of the Reforms, thus set back the clock of progress. (9) However pure my motives may be, those of the Mussalmans are obviously revengeful.

I shall now answer the objections in the order in which they are stated--

(1) In my opinion the Turkish claim is not only not immoral and unjust, but it is highly equitable, if only because Turkey wants to retain what is her own. And the Mahomedan manifesto has definitely declared that whatever guarantees may be necessary to be taken for the protection of non-Muslim and non-Turkish races, should be taken so as to give the Christians theirs and the Arabs their self-government under the Turkish suzerainty.

(2) I do not believe the Turk to be weak, incapable or cruel. He is certainly disorganised and probably without good generalship. He has been obliged to fight against heavy odds. The argument of weakness, incapacity and cruelty one often hears quoted in connection with those from whom power is sought to be taken away. About the alleged massacres a proper commission has been asked for, but never granted. And in any case security can be taken against oppression.

(3) I have already stated that if I were not interested in the Indian Mahomedans, I would not interest myself in the welfare of the Turks any more than I am in that of the Austrians or the Poles. But I am bound as an Indian to share the sufferings and trial of fellow-Indians. If I deem the Mahomedan to be my brother. It is my duty to help him in his hour of peril to the best of my ability, if his cause commends itself to me as just.

(4) The fourth refers to the extent Hindus should join hands with the Mahomedans. It is therefore a matter of feeling and opinion. It is expedient to suffer for my Mahomedan brother to the utmost in a just cause and I should therefore travel with him along the whole road so long as the means employed by him are as honourable as his end. I cannot regulate the Mahomedan feeling. I must accept his statement that the Khilafat is with him a religious question in the sense that it binds him to reach the goal even at the cost of his own life.

(5) I do not consider non-co-operation to be a rebellion, because it is free from violence. In a larger sense all opposition to a Government measure

is a rebellion. In that sense, rebellion in a just cause is a duty, the extent of opposition being determined by the measure of the injustice done and felt.

(6) My experience of last year shows me that in spite of aberrations in some parts of India, the country was entirely under control that the influence of Satyagraha was profoundly for its good and that where violence did break out there were local causes that directly contributed to it. At the same time I admit that even the violence that did take place on the part of the people and the spirit of lawlessness that was undoubtedly shown in some parts should have remained under check. I have made ample acknowledgment of the miscalculation I then made. But all the painful experience that I then gained did not any way shake my belief in Satyagraha or in the possibility of that matchless force being utilised in India. Ample provision is being made this time to avoid the mistakes of the past. But I must refuse to be deterred from a clear course; because it may be attended by violence totally unintended and in spite of extraordinary efforts that are being made to prevent it. At the same time I must make my position clear. Nothing can possibly prevent a Satyagrahi from doing his duty because of the frown of the authorities. I would risk, if necessary, a million lives so long as they are voluntary sufferers and are innocent, spotless victims. It is the mistakes of the people that matter in a Satyagraha campaign. Mistakes, even insanity must be expected from the strong and the powerful, and the moment of victory has come when there is no retort to the mad fury of the powerful, but a voluntary, dignified and quiet submission but not submission to the will of the authority that has put itself in the wrong. The secret of success lies therefore in holding every English life and the life of every officer serving the Government as sacred as those of our own dear ones. All the wonderful experience I have gained now during nearly 40 years of conscious existence, has convinced me that there is no gift so precious as that of life. I make bold to say that the moment the Englishmen feel that although they are in India in a hopeless minority, their lives are protected against harm not because of the matchless weapons of destruction which are at their disposal, but because Indians refuse to take the lives even of those whom they may consider to be utterly in the wrong that moment will see a transformation in the English nature in its relation to India and that moment will also be the moment when all the destructive cutlery that is to be had in India will begin to rust. I know that this is a far-off vision. That cannot matter to me. It is enough for me to see the light and to act up to it, and it is more than enough when I gain companions in the onward march. I have claimed in private conversations with English friends that it is because of my incessant preaching of the gospel of non-violence

and my having successfully demonstrated its practical utility that so far the forces of violence, which are undoubtedly in existence in connection with the Khilafat movement, have remained under complete control.

(7) From a religious standpoint the seventh objection is hardly worth considering. If people do not respond to the movement of non-co-operation, it would be a pity, but that can be no reason for a reformer not to try. It would be to me a demonstration that the present position of hopefulness is not dependent on any inward strength or knowledge, but it is hope born of ignorance and superstition.

(8) If non-co-operation is taken up in earnest, it must bring about a cessation of all other activities including the Reforms, but I decline to draw therefore the corollary that it will set back the clock of progress. On the contrary, I consider non-co-operation to be such a powerful and pure instrument, that if it is enforced in an earnest spirit, it will be like seeking first the Kingdom of God and everything else following as a matter of course. People will have then realised their true power. They would have learnt the value of discipline, self-control, joint action, non-violence, organisation and everything else that goes to make a nation great and good, and not merely great.

(9) I do not know that I have a right to arrogate greater purity for myself than for our Mussalman brethren. But I do admit that they do not believe in my doctrine of non-violence to the full extent. For them it is a weapon of the weak, an expedient. They consider non-co-operation without violence to be the only thing open to them in the war of direct action. I know that if some of them could offer successful violence, they would do to-day. But they are convinced that humanly speaking it is an impossibility. For them, therefore, non-co-operation is a matter not merely of duty but also of revenge. Whereas I take up non-co-operation against the Government as I have actually taken it up in practice against members of my own family. I entertain very high regard for the British constitution, I have not only no enmity against Englishmen but I regard much in English character as worthy of my emulation. I count many as my friends. It is against my religion to regard any one as an enemy. I entertain similar sentiments with respect to Mahomedans. I find their cause to be just and pure. Although therefore their viewpoint is different from mine I do not hesitate to associate with them and invite them to give my method a trial, for, I believe that the use of a pure weapon even from a mistaken motive does not fail to produce some good, even as the telling of truth if only because for the time being it is the best policy, is at least so much to the good.

MR. CANDLER'S OPEN LETTER

Mr. Candler has favoured me with an open letter on this question of questions. The letter has already appeared in the Press. I can appreciate Mr. Candler's position as I would like him and other Englishmen to appreciate mine and that of hundreds of Hindus who feel as I do. Mr. Candler's letter is an attempt to show that Mr. Lloyd George's pledge is not in any way broken by the peace terms. I quite agree with him that Mr. Lloyd George's words ought not to be torn from their context to support the Mahomedan claim. These are Mr. Lloyd George's words as quoted in the recent Viceregal message: "Nor are we fighting to destroy Austria-Hungary or to deprive Turkey of its capital or of the rich and renowned lands of Asia Minor and Thrace which are predominantly Turkish in race." Mr. Candler seems to read 'which', as if it meant 'if they,' whereas I give the pronoun its natural meaning, namely, that the Prime Minister knew in 1918, that the lands referred to by him were "predominantly Turkish in race." And if this is the meaning I venture to suggest that the pledge has been broken in a most barefaced manner, for there is practically nothing left to the Turk of 'the rich and renowned lands of Asia Minor and Thrace.'

I have already my view of the retention of the Sultan in Constantinople. It is an insult to the intelligence of man to suggest that 'the maintenance of the Turkish Empire in the homeland of the Turkish race with its capital at Constantinople has been left unimpaired by the terms of peace. This is the other passage from the speech which I presume Mr. Candler wants me to read together with the one already quoted:--

> "While we do not challenge the maintenance of the Turkish Empire in the home-land of the Turkish race with its capital at Constantinople, the passage between the Mediterranean and the Black Sea being inter-nationalised, Armenia, Mesopotamia, Syria and Palestine are in our judgment entitled to a recognition of their separate national condition."

Did that mean entire removal of Turkish influence, extinction of Turkish suzerainty and the introduction of European-Christian influence under the guise of Mandates? Have the Moslems of Arabia, Armenia, Mesopotamia, Syria and Palestine been committed, or is the new arrangement being superimposed upon them by Powers conscious of their own brute-strength rather than of justice of their action? I for one would nurse by every legitimate means the spirit of independence in the brave Arabs, but I shudder to think what will happen to them under the schemes of exploitation of their country by the greedy capitalists protected as they will be by the mandatory Powers. If the pledge is to be fulfilled, let these places have full self-government with suzerainty to be retained with Turkey as has been suggested by the

Times of India

. Let there be all the necessary guarantees taken from Turkey about the internal independence of the Arabs. But to remove that suzerainty, to deprive the Khalif of the wardenship of the Holy Places is to render Khilafat a mockery which no Mahomedan can possibly look upon with equanimity, I am not alone in my interpretation of the pledge. The Right Hon'ble Ameer Ali calls the peace terms a breach of faith. Mr. Charles Roberts reminds the British public that the Indian Mussalman sentiment regarding the Turkish Treaty is based upon the Prime Minister's pledge "regarding Thrace, Constantinople and Turkish lands in Asia Minor, repeated on February 26 last with deliberation by Mr. Lloyd George. Mr. Roberts holds that the pledge must be treated as a whole, not as binding only regarding Constantinople but also binding as regards Thrace and Asia Minor. He describes the pledge as binding upon the nation as a whole and its breach in any part as a gross breach of faith on the part of the British Empire. He demands that if there is an unanswerable reply to the charge of breach of faith it ought to be given and adds the Prime Minister may regard his own word lightly if he chooses, but he has no right to break a pledge given on behalf of the nation. He concludes that it is incredible that such pledge should not have been kept in the letter and in the spirit." He adds: "I have reason to believe that these views are fully shared by prominent members of the Cabinet."

I wonder if Mr. Candler knows what is going on to-day in England. Mr. Pickthall writing in *New Age* says: "No impartial international enquiry into the whole question of the Armenian massacres has been instituted in the ample time which has elapsed since the conclusion of armistice with Turkey. The Turkish Government has asked for such enquiry. But the Armenian organisations and the Armenian partisans refuse to hear of such a thing, declaring that the Bryce and Lepssens reports are quite sufficient to condemn the Turks. In other words the judgment should be given on the case for prosecution alone. The inter-allied commission which investigated the unfortunate events in Smyrna last year, made a report unfavourable to Greek claims. Therefore, that report has not been published here in England, though in other countries it has long been public property." He then goes on to show how money is being scattered by Armenian and Greek emissaries in order to popularise their cause and adds: "This conjunction of dense ignorance and cunning falsehood is fraught with instant danger to the British realm," and concludes: "A Government and people which prefer propaganda to fact as the ground of policy--and foreign policy at that--is self-condemned."

I have reproduced the above extract in order to show that the present British policy has been affected by propaganda of an unscrupulous nature.

Turkey which was dominant over two million square miles of Asia, Africa and Europe in the 17th century, under the terms of the treaty, says the *London Chronicle*, has dwindled down to little more than 1,000 square miles. It says, "All European Turkey could now be accommodated comfortably between the Landsend and the Tamar, Cornawal alone exceeding its total area and but for its alliance with Germany, Turkey could have been assured of retaining at least sixty thousand square miles of the Eastern Balkans." I do not know whether the *Chronicle* view is generally shared. Is it by way of punishment that Turkey is to undergo such shrinkage, or is it because justice demands it? If Turkey had not made the mistake of joining Germany, would the principle of nationality have been still applied to Armenia, Arabia, Mesopotamia and Palestine?

Let me now remind those who think with Mr. Candler that the promise was not made by Mr. Lloyd George to the people of India in anticipation of the supply of recruits continuing. In defending his own statement Mr. Lloyd George is reported to have said:

> "The effect of the statement in India was that recruiting went up appreciably from that very moment. They were not all Mahomedans but there were many Mahomedans amongst them. Now we are told that was an offer to Turkey. But they rejected it, and therefore we were absolutely free. It was not. It is too often forgotten that we are the greatest Mahomedan power in the world and one-fourth of the population of the British Empire is Mahomedan. There have been no more loyal adherents to the throne and no more effective and loyal supporters of the Empire in its hour of trial. *We gave a solemn pledge and they accepted it.* They are disturbed by the prospect of our not abiding by it."

Who shall interpret that pledge and how? How did the Government of India itself interpret it? Did it or did it not energetically support the claim for the control of the Holy Places of Islam vesting in the Khalif? Did the Government of India suggest that the whole of Jazirat-ul-Arab could be taken away consistently with that pledge from the sphere of influence of the Khalif, and given over to the Allies as mandatory Powers? Why does the Government of India sympathise with the Indian Mussalmans if the terms are all they should be? So much for the pledge. I would like to guard myself against being understood that I stand or fall absolutely by Mr. Lloyd George's declaration. I have advisedly used the adverb 'practically' in connection with it. It is an important qualification.'

Mr. Candler seems to suggest that my goal is something more than merely attaining justice on the Khilafat. If so, he is right. Attainment of justice is undoubtedly the corner-stone, and if I found that I was wrong in my conception of justice on this question, I hope I shall have the courage immediately to retrace my steps. But by helping the Mahomedans of India at a critical moment in their history, I want to buy their friendship. Moreover, if I can carry the Mahomedans with me I hope to wean Great Britain from the downward path along which the Prime Minister seems to me to be taking her. I hope also to show to India and the Empire at large that given a certain amount of capacity for self-sacrifice, justice can be secured by peacefullest and cleanest means without sowing or increasing bitterness between English and Indians. For, whatever may be the temporary effect of my methods, I know enough of them to feel certain that they alone are immune from lasting bitterness. They are untainted with hatred, expedience or untruth.

IN PROCESS OF KEEPING

The writer of 'Current Topics' in the "Times of India" has attempted to challenge the statement made in my Khilafat article regarding ministerial pledges, and in doing so cites Mr. Asquith's Guild-Hall speech of November 10, 1914. When I wrote the articles, I had in mind Mr. Asquith's speech. I am sorry that he ever made that speech. For, in my humble opinion, it betrayed to say the least, a confusion of thought. Could he think of the Turkish people as apart from the Ottoman Government? And what is the meaning of the death-knell of Ottoman Dominion in Europe and Asia if it be not the death knell of Turkish people as a free and governing race? Is it, again, true historically that the Turkish rule has always been a blight that 'has withered some of the fairest regions of the earth?' And what is the meaning of his statement that followed, viz., "Nothing is further from our thoughts than to imitate or encourage a crusade against their belief?" If words have any meaning, the qualifications that Mr. Asquith introduced in his speech should have meant a scrupulous regard for Indian Muslim feeling. And if that be the meaning of his speech, without anything further to support me I would claim that even Mr. Asquith's assurance is in danger of being set at nought if the resolutions of the San Remo Conference are to be crystallised into action. But I base remarks on a considered speech made by Mr. Asquith's successor two years later when things had assumed a more threatening shape than in 1914 and when the need for Indian help was much greater than in 1914. His pledge would bear repetition till it is fulfilled. He said: "Nor are we fighting to deprive Turkey of its capital or of the rich and renowned lands of Asia Minor and Thrace which are predominantly Turkish in race. We do not challenge the maintenance of the Turkish Empire in the homelands of the Turkish race with its capital at Constantinople." If only every word of this pledge is fulfilled both in letter and in spirit, there would be little left for quarrelling about. In so far as Mr. Asquith's declaration can be considered hostile to the Indian Muslim claim, it its superseded by the later and more considered declaration of Mr. Lloyd George--a declaration made irrevocable by fulfilment of the consideration it expected, viz. the enlistment of the brave Mahomedan soldiery which fought in the very place which is now being partitioned in spite of the pledge. But the writer of 'Current Topics' says Mr. Lloyd George "is now in process of keeping his pledge" I hope he is right. But what has already happened gives little ground for any such hope. For, imprisonment or internment of the Khalif in his own capital will be not only a mockery of fulfilment but it would he adding injury to insult. Either the Turkish Empire is to be maintained in the homelands of the Turkish race with its capital at Constantinople or it is not. If it is, let the Indian Mahomedans feel the full glow of it or if the Empire is to be broken up, let the mask of hypocrisy be lifted and India see the truth in its nakedness. To join the Khilafat movement then means to join a movement to keep inviolate the pledge of a British minister. Surely, such a movement is worth much greater sacrifice than may be involved in non-co-operation.

APPEAL TO THE VICEROY

Your Excellency.

As one who has enjoyed a certain measure of your Excellency's confidence, and as one who claims to be a devoted well-wisher of the British Empire, I owe it to your Excellency, and through your Excellency to His Majesty's Ministers, to explain my connection with and my conduct in the Khilafat question.

At the very earliest stages of the war, even whilst I was in London organising the Indian Volunteer Ambulance Corps, I began to interest myself in the Khilafat question. I perceived how deeply moved the little Mussalman World in London was when Turkey decided to throw in her lot with Germany. On my arrival in India in the January of 1915, I found the same anxiousness and earnestness among the Mussalmans with whom I came in contact. Their anxiety became intense when the information about the Secret Treaties leaked out. Distrust of British intentions filled their minds, and despair took possession of them. Even at that moment I advised my Mussalman friends not to give way to despair, but to express their fear and their hopes in a disciplined manner. It will be admitted that the whole of Mussalman India has behaved in a singularly restrained manner during the past five years and that the leaders have been able to keep the turbulent sections of their community under complete control.

The peace terms and your Excellency's defence of them have given the Mussalmans of India a shock from which it will be difficult for them to recover. The terms violate ministerial pledges and utterly disregard

Mussalman sentiment. I consider that as a staunch Hindu wishing to live on terms of the closest friendship with my Mussalman countrymen. I should be an unworthy son of India if I did not stand by them in their hour of trial. In my humble opinion their cause is just. They claim that Turkey must be *punished* if their sentiment is to be respected. Muslim soldiers did fight to inflict punishment on their own Khalifa or to deprive him of his territories. The Mussalman attitude has been consistent, throughout these five years.

My duty to the Empire to which I owe my loyalty requires me to resist the cruel violence that has been done to the Mussalman sentiment. So far as I am aware, Mussulmans and Hindus have as a whole lost faith in British justice and honour. The report of the majority of the Hunter Committee, Your Excellency's despatch thereon and Mr. Montagu's reply have only aggravated the distrust.

In these circumstances the only course open to one like me is either in despair to sever all connection with British rule, or, if I still retained faith in the inherent superiority of the British constitution to all others at present in vogue to adopt such means as will rectify the wrong done, and thus restore confidence. I have not lost faith in such superiority and I am not without hope that somehow or other justice will yet be rendered if we show the requisite capacity for suffering. Indeed, my conception of that constitution is that it helps only those who are ready to help themselves. I do not believe that it protects the weak. It gives free scope to the strong to maintain their strength and develop it. The weak under it go to the wall.

It is, then, because I believe in the British constitution that I have advised my Mussalman friends to withdraw their support from your Excellency's Government and the Hindus to join them, should the peace terms not be revised in accordance with the solemn pledges of Ministers and the Muslim sentiment.

Three courses were open to the Mahomedans in order to mark their emphatic disapproval of the utter injustice to which His Majesty's Ministers have become party, if they have not actually been the prime perpetrators of it. They are:--

(1) To resort to violence,

(2) To advise emigration on a wholesale scale,

(3) Not to be party to the injustice by ceasing to co-operate with the Government.

Your Excellency must be aware that there was a time when the boldest, though the most thoughtless among the Mussulmans favoured violence, and the "Hijrat" (emigration) has not yet ceased to be the battle-cry. I venture to claim that I have succeeded by patient reasoning in weaning the party of violence from its ways. I confess that I did not--I did not attempt to succeed in weaning them from violence on moral grounds, but purely on utilitarian grounds. The result, for the time being at any has, however, been to stop violence. The School of "Hijrat" has received a check, if it has not stopped its activity entirely. I hold that no repression could have prevented a violent eruption, if the people had not had presented to them a form of direct action involving considerable sacrifice and ensuring success if such direct action was largely taken up by the public. Non-co-operation was the only dignified and constitutional form of such direct action. For it is the right recognised from times immemorial of the subject to refuse to assist a ruler who misrules.

At the same time I admit that non-co-operation practised by the mass of people is attended with grave risks. But, in a crisis such as has overtaken the Mussalmans of India, no step that is unattended with large risks, can possibly bring about the desired change. Not to run some risks now will be to court much greater risks if not virtual destruction of Law and Order.

But there is yet an escape from non-co-operation. The Mussalman representation has requested your Excellency to lead the agitation yourself, as did your distinguished predecessor at the time of the South African trouble. But if you cannot see your way to do so, and non-co-operation becomes a dire necessity, I hope that your Excellency will give those who have accepted my advice and myself the credit for being actuated by nothing less than a stern sense of duty.

I have the honour to remain,

Your Excellency's faithful servant, (Sd.) M.K. GANDHI. Laburnam Road, Gamdevi, Bombay 22nd June 1920

THE PREMIER'S REPLY

The English mail has brought us a full and official report of the Premier's speech which he recently made when he received the Khilafat deputation. Mr. Lloyd George's speech is more definite and therefore more disappointing than H.E. the Viceroy's reply to the deputation here. He draws quite unwarranted deductions from the same high principles on which he had based his own pledge only two years ago. He declares that Turkey must pay the penalty of defeat. This determination to punish Turkey does not become one whose immediate predecessor had, in order to appease Muslim soldiers, promised that the British Government had no designs on Turkey and that His Majesty's Government would never think of punishing the Sultan for the misdeeds of the Turkish Committee. Mr. Lloyd George has expressed his belief that the majority of the population of Turkey did not really want to quarrel with Great Britain and that their rulers misled the country. In spite of this conviction and in spite of Mr. Asquith's promise, he is out to punish Turkey and punish it in the name of justice.

He expounds the principle of self-determination and justifies the scheme of depriving Turkey of its territories one after another. While justifying this scheme he does not exclude even Thrace and this strikes the reader most, because this very Thrace he had mentioned in his pledge as predominantly Turkish. Now we are told by him that both the Turkish census and the Greek census agree in pointing out the Mussulman population in Thrace is in a considerable minority! Mr. Yakub Hussain speaking at the Madras Khilafat conference has challenged the truth of this statement. The Prime Minister cites among others also the example of Smyrna where, he says, we had a most careful investigation by a very impartial committee in the whole of the question of Smyrna and it was found that considerable majority was non-Turkish.' Who will believe the one-sided "impartial committee's" investigations until it is disproved that thousands of Musselmans have been murdered and hundreds of thousands have been driven away from their hearths and homes? Strangely enough Mr. Lloyd George, believes in the necessity of fresh investigations by a purposely appointed committee in Smyrna as the most authenticated and up-to-date report, whereas he would not accept Mr. Mahomed Ali's proposal for an impartial commission in regard to Armenian massacre! Doubtful and one-sided facts and figures suffice for him even to conclude that the Turkish Government is incapable of protecting its subjects. And he proceeds to suggest foreign interference in ruling over Asia Minor in the interests of civilization. Here he cuts at the root of the Sultan's independence. This proposal of appropriating supervision is distinctly unlike the treatment meted out to other enemy powers.

This detraction of the Sultan's suzerainty is only a corollary of the Premier's indifference towards the Muslim idea of the Caliphate. The premier's injustice in treating the Turkish question becomes graver when he thus lightly handles the Khilafat question. There had been occasions when the British have used to their advantage the Muslim idea of associating the Caliph's spiritual power with temporal power. Now this very association is treated as a controversial question by the great statesman.

Will this raise the reputation of Great Britain or stain it? Can this be tolerated by those who fought against Turkey with full faith in British honesty? Mere receipts of gratitude cannot console the wounded Mussalmans. There lies the alternative for England to choose between two mandates--a mandate over some Turkish territories which is sure to lead to chaos all over the world and a mandate over the hearts of the Muhomedans which will redeem the pledged honour of Britain. The prime minister has an unwise choice. This narrow view registers the latest temperature of British diplomacy.

THE MUSSULMAN REPRESENTATION

Slowly but surely the Mussulmans are preparing for the battle before them. They have to fight against odds that are undoubtedly heavy but not half as heavy as the prophet had against him. How often did he not put his life in danger? But his faith in God was unquenchable. He went forward with a light heart, for God was on his side, for he represented truth. If his followers have half the prophet's faith and half his spirit of sacrifice, the odds will be presently even and will in little while turn against the despoilers of Turkey. Already the rapacity of the Allies is telling against themselves. France finds her task difficult. Greece cannot stomach her ill-gotten gains. And England finds Mesopotamia a tough job. The oil of Mosul may feed the fire she has so wantonly lighted and burn her fingers badly. The newspapers say the Arabs do not like the presence of the Indian soldiery in their midst. I do not wonder. They are a fierce and a brave people and do not understand why Indian soldiers should find themselves in Mesopotamia. Whatever the fate of non-co-operation, I wish that not a single Indian will offer his services for Mesopotamia whether for the civil or the military department. We must learn to think for ourselves and before entering upon any employment find out whether thereby we may not make ourselves instruments of injustice. Apart from the question of Khilafat and from the point of abstract justice the English have no right to hold Mesopotamia. It is no part of our loyalty to help the Imperial Government in what is in plain language daylight robbery. If therefore we seek civil or military employment in Mesopotamia we do so for the sake of earning a livelihood. It is our duty to see that the source is not tainted.

It surprises me to find so many people shirking over the mention of non-co-operation. There is no instrument so clean, so harmless and yet so effective as non-co-operation. Judiciously hauled it need not produce any evil consequences. And its intensity will depend purely on the capacity of the people for sacrifice.

The chief thing is to prepare the atmosphere of non-co-operation. "We are not going to co-operate with you in your injustice," is surely the right and the duty of every intelligent subject to say. Were it not for our utter servility, helplessness and want of confidence in ourselves, we would certainly grasp this clean weapon and make the most effective use of it. Even the most despotic government cannot stand except for the consent of the governed which consent is often forcibly procured by the despot.

Immediately the subject ceases to fear the despotic force his power is gone. But the British government is never and nowhere entirely or laid upon force. It does make an honest attempt to secure the goodwill of the governed. But it does not hesitate to adopt unscrupulous means to compel the consent of the governed. It has not gone beyond the 'Honesty is the best policy' idea. It therefore bribes you into consenting its will by awarding titles, medals and ribbons, by giving you employment, by its superior financial ability to open for its employees avenues for enriching themselves and finally when these fail, it resorts to force. That is what Sir Michael O'Dwyer did and that is almost every British administrator will certainly do if he thought it necessary. If then we would not be greedy, if we would not run after titles and medals and honorary posts which do the country no good, half the battle is won.

My advisers are never tired of telling me that even if the Turkish peace terms are revised it will not be due to non-co-operation. I venture to suggest to them that non-co-operation has a higher purpose than mere revision of the terms. If I cannot compel revision I must at least cease to support a government that becomes party to the usurpation. And if I succeed in pushing non-co-operation to the extreme limit, I do compel the Government to choose between India and the usurpation. I have faith enough in England to know that at that moment England will expel her present jaded ministers and put in others who will make a clean sweep of the terms in consultation with an awakened India, draft terms that will be honourable to her, to Turkey and acceptable to India. But I hear my critics say "India has not the strength of purpose and the capacity for the sacrifice to achieve such a noble end. They are partly right. India has not these qualities now, because we have not--shall we not evolve them and infect the nation with them? Is not the attempt worth making? Is my sacrifice too great to gain such a great purpose?"

CRITICISM OF THE MUSLIM MANIFESTO

The Khilafat representation addressed to the Viceroy and my letter on the same subject have been severely criticised by the Anglo-Indian press.

The Times of India

which generally adopts an impartial attitude has taken strong exception to certain statements made in the Muslim manifesto and has devoted a paragraph of its article to an advance criticism of my suggestion that His Excellency should resign if the peace terms are not revised.

The Times of India excepts to the submission that the British Empire may not treat Turkey like a departed enemy. The signatories have, I think, supplied the best of reasons. They say "We respectfully submit that in the treatment of Turkey the British Government are bound to respect Indian Muslim sentiment in so far as it is neither unjust nor unreasonable." If the seven crore Mussulmans are partners in the Empire, I submit that their wish must be held to be all sufficient for refraining from punishing Turkey. It is beside the point to quote what Turkey did during the war. It has suffered for it. *The Times* inquires wherein Turkey has been treated worse than the other Powers. I thought that the fact was self-evident. Neither Germany nor Austria and Hungary has been treated in the same way that Turkey has been. The whole of the Empire has been reduced to the retention of a portion of its capital, as it were, to mock the Sultan and that too has been done under terms so humiliating that no self-respecting person much less a reigning sovereign can possibly accept.

The Times has endeavoured to make capital out of the fact that the representation does not examine the reason for Turkey not joining the Allies. Well there was no mystery about it. The fact of Russia being one of the Allies was enough to warn Turkey against joining them. With Russia knocking at the gate at the time of the war it was not an easy matter for Turkey to join the Allies. But Turkey had cause to suspect Great Britain herself. She knew that England had done no friendly turn to her during the Bulgarian War. She was hardly well served at the time of the war with Italy. It was still no doubt a bad choice. With the Musssalmans of India awakened and ready to support her, her statesmen might have relied upon Britain not being allowed to damage Turkey if she had remained with the Allies. But this is all wisdom after event. Turkey made a bad choice and she was punished for it. To humiliate her now is to ignore the Indian Mussulman sentiment. Britain may not do it and retain the loyalty of the awakened Mussulmans of India.

For "The Times" to say that the peace terms strictly follow the principle of self-determination is to throw dust in the eyes of its readers. Is it the principle of self-determination that has caused the cessation of Adrianople and Thrace to Greece? By what principle of self-determination has Smyrna been handed to Greece? Have the inhabitants of Thrace and Smyrna asked for Grecian tutelege?

I decline to believe that the Arabs like the disposition that has been made of them. Who is the King of Hedjaj and who is Emir Feisul? Have the Arabs elected these kings and chiefs? Do the Arabs like the Mandate being taken by England? By the time the whole thing is finished, the very name self-determination will stink in one's nostrils. Already signs are not wanting to show that the Arabs, the Thracians and the Smyrnans are resenting their disposal. They may not like Turkish rule but they like the present arrangement less. They could have made their own honourable terms with Turkey but these self-determining people will now be held down by the 'matchless might' of the allied *i.e.,* British forces. Britain had the straight course open to her of keeping the Turkish Empire intact and taking sufficient guarantees for good government. But her Prime Minister chose the crooked course of secret treaties, duplicity and hypocritical subterfuges.

There is still a way out. Let her treat India as a real partner. Let her call the true representatives of the Mussalmans. Let them go to Arabia and the other parts of the Turkish Empire and let her devise a scheme that would not humiliate Turkey, that would satisfy the just Muslim sentiment and that will secure honest self-determination for the races composing that Empire. If it was Canada, Australia or South Africa that had to be placated, Mr. Lloyd George would not have dared to ignore them. They have the power to secede. India has not. Let him no more insult India by calling her a partner, if her feelings count for naught. I invite *The Times of India* to reconsider its position and join an honourable agitation in which a high-souled people are seeking nothing but justice.

I do with all deference still suggest that the least that Lord Chelmsford can do is to resign if the sacred feelings of India's sons are not to be consulted and respected by the Ministers. *The Times* is over-taxing the constitution when it suggests that as a constitutional Viceroy it is not open to Lord Chelmsford to go against the decision of his Majesty's Ministers. It is certainly not open to a Viceroy to retain office and oppose ministerial decisions. But the constitution does allow a Viceroy to resign his high office when he is called upon to carry out decisions that are immoral as the peace terms are or like these terms are calculated to stir to their very depth the feelings of those whose affair he is administering for the time being.

THE MAHOMEDAN DECISION

The Khilafat meeting at Allahabad has unanimously reaffirmed the principle of non-co-operation and appointed an executive committee to lay down and enforce a detailed programme. This meeting was preceded by a joint Hindu-Mahomedan meeting at which Hindu leaders were invited to give their views. Mrs. Beasant, the Hon'ble Pandit Malaviyuji, the Hon'ble Dr. Sapru Motilal Nehru Chintamani and others were present at the meeting. It was a wise step on the part of the Khilafat Committee to invite Hindus representing all shades of thought to give them the benefit of their advice. Mrs. Besant and Dr. Sapru strongly dissuaded the Mahomedans present from the policy of non-co-operation. The other Hindu speakers made non-committal speeches. Whilst the other Hindu speakers approved of the principle of non-co-operation in theory, they saw many practical difficulties and they feared also complications arising from Mahomedans welcoming an Afghan invasion of India. The Mahomedan speakers gave the fullest and frankest assurances that they would fight to a man any invader who wanted to conquer India, but were equally frank in asserting that any invasion from without undertaken with a view to uphold the prestige of Islam and to vindicate justice would have their full sympathy if not their actual support. It is easy enough to understand and justify the Hindu caution. It is difficult to resist Mahomedan position. In my opinion, the best way to prevent India from becoming the battle ground between the forces of Islam and those of the English is for Hindus to make non-co-operation a complete and immediate success, and I have little doubt that if the Mahomedans remain true to their declared intention and are able to exercise self-restraint, and make sacrifices the Hindus will "play the game" and join them in the campaign of non-co-operation. I feel equally certain that the Hindus will not assist Mahomedans in promoting or bringing about an armed conflict between the British Government and their allies, and Afghanistan. British forces are too well organised to admit of any successful invasion of the Indian frontier. The only way, therefore, the Mahomedans can carry on an effective struggle on behalf of the honour of Islam is to take up non-co-operation in real earnest. It will not only be completely effective if it is adopted by the people on an extensive scale, but it will also provide full scope for individual conscience. If I cannot bear an injustice done by an individual or a corporation, and if I am directly or indirectly instrumental in upholding that individual or corporation, I must answer for it before my Maker, but I have done all it is humanly possible for me to do consistently with the moral code that refuses to injure even the wrong-doer, if I cease to support the injustice in the manner described above. In applying therefore such a great force there should be no haste, there should be no temper shown. Non-co-operation must be and remain absolutely a voluntary effort. The whole thing then depends upon Mahomedans themselves. If they will but help themselves Hindu help will come and the Government, great and mighty though it is, will have to bend before this irresistible force. No Government can possibly withstand the bloodless opposition of a whole nation.

MR. ANDREWS' DIFFICULTY

Mr. Andrews whose love for India is equalled only by his love for England and whose mission in life is to serve God, i.e., humanity through India, has contributed remarkable articles to the 'Bombay Chronicle' on the Khilafat movement. He has not spared England, France or Italy. He has shown how Turkey has been most unjustly dealt with and how the Prime Minister's pledge has been broken. He has devoted the last article to an examination of Mr. Mahomed Ali's letter to the Sultan and has come to the conclusion that Mr. Mahomed Ali's statement of claim is at variance with the claim set forth in the latest Khilafat representation to the Viceroy which he wholly approves.

Mr. Andrews and I have discussed the question as fully as it was possible. He asked me publicly to define my own position more fully than I have done. His sole object in inviting discussion is to give strength to a cause which he holds as intrinsically just, and to gather round it the best opinion of Europe so that the allied powers and especially England may for very shame be obliged to revise the terms.

I gladly respond to Mr. Andrew's invitation. I should clear the ground by stating that I reject any religious doctrine that does not appeal to reason and is in conflict with morality. I tolerate unreasonable religious sentiment when it is not immoral. I hold the Khilafat claim to be both just and reasonable and therefore it derives greater force because it has behind it the religious sentiment of the Mussalman world.

In my opinion Mr. Mahomed Ali's statement is unexceptionable. It is no doubt clothed in diplomatic language. But I am not prepared to quarrel with the language so long as it is sound in substance.

Mr. Andrews considers that Mr. Mahomed Ali's language goes to show that he would resist Armenian independence against the Armenians and the Arabian against the Arabs. I attach no such meaning to it. What he, the whole of Mussalmans and therefore I think also the Hindus resist is the shameless attempt of England and the other Powers under cover of self-determination to emasculate and dismember Turkey. If I understand the spirit of Islam properly, it is essentially republican in the truest sense of the term. Therefore if Armenia or Arabia desired independence of Turkey they should have it. In the case of Arabia, complete Arabian independence would mean transference of the Khilafat to an Arab chieftain. Arabia in that sense is a Mussulman trust, not purely Arabian. And the Arabs without ceasing to be Mussulman, could not hold Arabia against Muslim opinion. The Khalifa must be the custodian of the Holy places and therefore also the routes to them. He must be able to defend them against the whole world. And if an Arab chief arose who could better satisfy that test than the Sultan of Turkey, I have no doubt that he would be recognised as the Khalifa.

I have thus discussed the question academically. The fact is that neither the Mussulmans nor the Hindus believe in the English Ministerial word. They do not believe that the Arabs or the Armenians want complete independence of Turkey. That they want self-government is beyond doubt.

Nobody disputes that claim. But nobody has ever ascertained that either the Arabs or the Armenians desire to do away with all connection, even nominal, with Turkey.

The solution of the question lies not in our academic discussion of the ideal position, it lies in an honest appointment of a mixed commission of absolutely independent Indian Mussulmans and Hindus and independent Europeans to investigate the real wish of the Armenians and the Arabs and then to come to a *modus vivendi* where by the claims of the nationality and those of Islam may be adjusted and satisfied.

It is common knowledge that Smyrna and Thrace including Adrianople have been dishonestly taken away from Turkey and that mandates have been unscrupulously established in Syria and Mesopotamia and a British nominee has been set up in Hedjaj under the protection of British guns. This is a position that is intolerable and unjust. Apart therefore from the questions of Armenia and Arabia, the dishonesty and hypocrisy that pollute the peace terms require to be instantaneously removed. It paves the way to an equitable solution of the question of Armenian and Arabian independence which in theory no one denies and which in practice may be easily guaranteed if only the wishes of the people concerned could with any degree of certainty be ascertained.

THE KHILAFAT AGITATION

A friend who has been listening to my speeches once asked me whether I did not come under the sedition section of the Indian Penal Code. Though I had not fully considered it, I told him that very probably I did and that I could not plead 'not guilty' if I was charged under it. For I must admit that I can pretend to no 'affection' for the present Government.

And my speeches are intended to create 'dis-affection' such that the people might consider it a shame to assist or co-operate with a Government that had forfeited all title to confidence, respect or support.

I draw no distinction between the Imperial and the Indian Government. The latter has accepted, on the Khilafat, the policy imposed upon it by the former. And in the Punjab case the former has endorsed the policy of terrorism and emasculation of a brave people initiated by the latter. British ministers have broken their pledged word and wantonly wounded the feelings of the seventy million Mussulmans of India. Innocent men and women were insulted by the insolent officers of the Punjab Government. Their wrongs not only remain unrighted but the very officers who so cruelly subjected them to barbarous humiliation retain office under the Government.

When at Amritsar last year I pleaded with all the earnestness I could command for co-operation with the Government and for response to the wishes expressed in the Royal Proclamation. I did so because I honestly believed that, a new era was about to begin, and that the old spirit of fear, distrust and consequent terrorism was about to give place to the new spirit of respect, trust and goodwill. I sincerely believed that the Mussulman sentiment would be placated and that the officers that had misbehaved during the Martial Law regime in the Punjab would be at least dismissed and the people would be otherwise made to feel that a Government that had always been found quick (and mighty) to punish popular excesses would not fail to punish its agents' misdeeds. But to my amazement and dismay I have discovered that the present representatives of the Empire have become dishonest and unscrupulous. They have no real regard for the wishes of the people of India and they count Indian honour as of little consequence.

I can no longer retain affection for a Government so evilly manned as it is now-a-days. And for me, it is humiliating to retain my freedom and be witness to the continuing wrong. Mr. Montagu however is certainly right in threatening me with deprivation of my liberty if I persist in endangering the existence of the Government. For that must be the result if my activity bears fruit. My only regret is that inasmuch as Mr. Montagu admits my past services, he might have perceived that there must be something exceptionally bad in the Government if a well-wisher like me could no longer give his affection to it. It was simpler to insist on justice being done to the Mussalmans and to the Punjab than to threaten me with punishment so that the injustice might be perpetuated. Indeed I fully expect it will be found that even in promoting disaffection towards an unjust Government I had rendered greater services to the Empire than I am already credited with.

At the present moment, however, the duty of those who approve my activity is clear. They ought on no account to resent the deprivation of my liberty, should the Government of India deem it to be their duty to take it away. A citizen has no right to resist such restriction imposed in accordance with the laws of the State to which he belongs. Much less have those who sympathise with him. In my case there can be no question of sympathy. For I deliberately oppose the Government to the extent of trying to put its very existence in jeopardy. For my supporters, therefore, it must be a moment of joy when I am imprisoned. It means the beginning of success if only the supporters continue the policy for which I stand. If the Government arrest me, they would do so in order to stop the progress of Non-co-operation which I preach. It follows that if Non-co-operation continues with unabated vigour, even after my arrest, the Government must imprison others or grant the people's wish in order to gain their co-operation. Any eruption of violence on the part of the people even under provocation would end in disaster. Whether therefore it is I or any one else who is arrested during the campaign, the first condition of success is that there must be no resentment shown against it. We cannot imperil the very existence of a Government and quarrel with its attempt to save itself by punishing those who place it in danger.

HIJARAT AND ITS MEANING

India is a continent. Its articulate thousands know what its inarticulate millions are doing or thinking. The Government and the educated Indians may think that the Khilafat movement is merely a passing phase. The millions of Mussalmans think otherwise. The flight of the Mussalmans is growing apace. The newspapers contain paragraphs in out of the way corners informing the readers that a special train containing a barrister with sixty women, forty children including twenty sucklings, all told 765, have left for Afghanistan. They were cheered *en route*. They were presented with cash, edibles and other things, and were joined by more Muhajarins on the way. No fanatical preaching by Shaukatali can make people break up and leave their homes for an unknown land. There must be an abiding faith in them. That it is better for them to leave a State which has no regard for their religious sentiment and face a beggar's life than to remain in it even though it may be in a princely manner. Nothing but pride of power can blind the Government of India to the scene that is being enacted before it.

But there is yet another side to the movement. Here are the facts as stated in the following Government *Communique* dated 10th July 1920:--

> An unfortunate affair in connection with the Mahajarin occurred on the 8th instant at Kacha Garhi between Peshawar and Jamrud. The following are the facts as at present reported. Two members of a party of the Mahajarins proceeding by train to Jamrud were detected by the British military police travelling without tickets. Altercation ensued at Islamia College Station, but the train proceeded to Kacha Garhi. An attempt was made to evict these Mahajarins, whereupon the military police were attacked by a crowd of some forty Mahajarins and the British officer who intervened was seriously wounded with a spade. A detachment of Indian troops at Kacha Garhi thereupon fired two or three shots at the Mahajarin for making murderous assault on the British officer. One Mahajarin was killed and one wounded and three arrested. Both the military and the police were injured. The body of the Mahajarin was despatched to Peshawar and buried on the morning of the 9th. This incident

> has caused considerable excitement in Peshawar City, and the Khilafat Hijrat Committee are exercising restraining influence. Shops were closed on the morning of the 9th. A full enquiry has been instituted.

Now Peshawar to Jamrud is a matter of a few miles. It was clearly the duty of the military not to attempt to pull out the ticketless Mahajarins for the sake of a few annas. But they actually attempted force. Intervention by the rest of the party was a foregone conclusion. An altercation ensued. A British officer was attacked with a spade. Firing and a death of a Mahajarin was the result. Has British prestige been enhanced by the episode? Why have not the Government put tactful officers in charge at the frontier, whilst a great religious emigration is in progress? The action of the military will pass from tongue to tongue throughout India and the Mussalman world around, will not doubt be unconsciously and even consciously exaggerated in the passage and the feeling bitter as it already is will grow in bitterness. The

Communique

says that the Government are making further inquiry. Let us hope that it will be full and that better arrangements will be made to prevent a repetition of what appears to have been a thoughtless act on the part of the military.

And may I draw the attention of those who are opposing non-co-operation that unless they find out a substitute they should either join the non-co-operation movement or prepare to face a disorganised subterranean upheaval whose effect no one can foresee and whose spread it would be impossible to check or regulate?

III-THE PUNJAB WRONGS

POLITICAL FREEMASONRY

Freemasonry is a secret brotherhood which has more by its secret and iron rules than by its service to humanity obtained a hold upon some of the best minds. Similarly there seems to be some secret code of conduct governing the official class in India before which the flower of the great British nation fall prostrate and unconsciously become instruments of injustice which as private individuals they would be ashamed of perpetrating. In no other way is it possible for one to understand the majority report of the Hunter Committee, the despatch of the Government of India, and the reply thereto of the Secretary of State for India. In spite of the energetic protests of a section of the Press to the personnel of the committee, it might be said that on the whole the public were prepared to trust it especially as it contained three Indian members who could fairly be claimed to be independent. The first rude shock to this confidence was delivered by the refusal of Lord Hunter's Committee to accept the very moderate and reasonable demand of the Congress Committee that the imprisoned Punjab leaders might be allowed to appear before it to instruct Counsel. Any doubt that might have been left in the mind of any person has been dispelled by the report of the majority of that committee. The result has justified the attitude of the Congress Committee. The evidence collected by it shows what lord Hunter's Committee purposely denied itself.

The minority report stands out like an oasis in a desert. The Indian members deserve the congratulation of their countrymen for having dared to do their duty in the face of heavy odds. I wish that they had refused to associate themselves even in a modified manner with the condemnation of the civil disobedience form of Satyagraha. The defiant spirit of the Delhi mob on the 30th March 1919 can hardly be used for condemning a great spiritual movement which is admittedly and manifestly intended to restrain the violent tendencies of mobs and to replace criminal lawlessness by civil disobedience of authority, when it has forfeited all title to respect. On the 30th March civil disobedience had not even been started. Almost every great popular demonstration has been hitherto attended all the world over by a certain amount of lawlessness. The demonstration of 30th March and 6th April could have been held under any other aegis us under that of Satyagrah. I hold that without the advent of the spirit of civility and orderliness the disobedience would have taken a much more violent form than it did even at Delhi. It was only the wonderfully quick acceptance by the people of the principle of Satyagrah that effectively checked the spread of violence throughout the length and breadth of India. And even to-day it is not the memory of the black barbarity of General Dyer that is keeping the undoubted restlessness among the people from breaking forth into violence. The hold that Satyagrah has gained on the people--it may be even against their will--is curbing the forces of disorder and violence. But I must not detain the reader on a defence of Satyagrah against unjust attacks. If it has gained a foothold in India, it will survive much fiercer attacks than the one made by the majority of the Hunter Committee and somewhat supported by the minority. Had the majority report been defective only in this direction and correct in every other there would have been nothing but praise for it. After all Satyagrah is a new experiment in political field. And a hasty attributing to it of any popular disorder would have been pardonable.

The universally pronounced adverse judgment upon the report and the despatches rests upon far more painful revelations. Look at the manifestly laboured defence of every official act of inhumanity except where condemnation could not be avoided through the impudent admissions made by the actors themselves; look at the special pleading introduced to defend General Dyer even against himself; look at the vain glorification of Sir Michael O'Dwyer although it was his spirit that actuated every act of criminality on the part of the subordinates; look at the deliberate refusal to examine his wild career before the events of April. His acts were an open book of which the committee ought to have taken judicial notices. Instead of accepting everything that the officials had to say, the Committee's obvious duty was to tax itself to find out the real cause of the disorders. It ought to have gone out of its way to search out the inwardness of the events. Instead of patiently going behind the hard crust of official documents, the Committee allowed itself to be guided with criminal laziness by mere official evidence. The report and the despatches, in my humble opinion, constitute an attempt to condone official lawlessness. The cautious and half-hearted condemnation pronounced upon General Dyer's massacre and the notorious crawling order only deepens the disappointment of the reader as he goes through page after page of thinly disguised official whitewash. I need, however, scarcely attempt any elaborate examination of the report or the despatches which have been so justly censured by the whole national press whether of the moderate or the extremist hue. The point to consider is how to break down this secret--be the secrecy over so unconscious--conspiracy to uphold official iniquity. A scandal of this magnitude cannot be tolerated by the nation, if it is to preserve its self-respect and become a free partner in the Empire. The All-India Congress Committee has resolved upon convening a special session of the Congress for the purpose of considering, among other things, the situation arising from the report. In my opinion the time has arrived when we must cease to rely upon mere petition to Parliament for effective action. Petitions will have value, when the nation has behind it the power to enforce its will. What power then have we? When we are firmly of opinion that grave wrong has been done us and when after an appeal to the highest authority we fail to secure redress, there must be some power available to us for undoing the wrong. It is true that in the vast majority of cases it is the duty of a subject to submit to wrongs on failure of the usual procedure, so long as they do not affect his vital being. But every nation and every individual has the right and it is their duty, to rise against an intolerable wrong. I do not believe in armed risings. They are a remedy worse than the disease sought to be cured. They are a token of the spirit of revenge and impatience and anger. The method of violence cannot do good in the long run. Witness the effect of the armed rising of the allied powers against Germany. Have they not become even like the Germans, as the latter have been depicted to us by them?

We have a better method. Unlike that of violence it certainly involves the exercise of restraint and patience: but it requires also resoluteness of will. This method is to refuse to be party to the wrong. No tyrant has ever yet succeeded in his purpose without carrying the victim with him, it may be, as it often is, by force. Most people choose rather to yield to the will of the tyrant than to suffer for the consequences of resistance. Hence does terrorism form part of the stock-in-trade of the tyrant. But we have instances in history where terrorism has failed to impose the terrorist's will upon his victim. India has the choice before her now. If then the acts of the Punjab Government be an insufferable wrong, if the report of Lord Hunter's Committee and the two despatches be a greater wrong by reason of their grievous condonation of those acts, it is clear that we must refuse to submit to this official violence. Appeal the Parliament by all means, if necessary, but if the Parliament fails us and if we are worthy to call ourselves a nation, we must refuse to uphold the Government by withdrawing co-operation from it.

THE DUTY OF THE PUNJABEE

The Allahabad

Leader

deserves to be congratulated for publishing the correspondence on Mr. Bosworth Smith who was one of the Martial Law officers against whom the complaints about persistent and continuous ill-treatment were among the bitterest. It appears from the correspondence that Mr. Bosworth Smith has received promotion instead of dismissal. Sometime before Martial Law Mr. Smith appears to have been degraded. "He has since been restored," says the

Leader

correspondent, "to his position of a Deputy Commissioner of the second grade from which he was degraded and also been invested with power under section 30 of the Criminal Procedure Code. Since his arrival, the poor Indian population of the town of Amhala Cantonment has been living under a regime of horror and tyranny." The correspondent adds: "I use both these words deliberately for conveying precisely what they mean." I cull a few passage from this illuminating letter to illustrate the meaning of horror and tyranny. "In private complaints he never takes the statement of the complainant. It is taken down by the reader when the court rises and got signed by the magistrate the following day. Whether the report received (upon such complaints) is favourable to the complainant or unfavourable to him, it is never ready by the magistrate, and complaints are dismissed without proper trial. This is the fate of private complaints. Now as regards police chellans. Pleaders for the accused are not allowed to interview under trial prisoners in police custody. They are not allowed to cross-examine prosecution witnesses.... Prosecution witnesses are examined with leading questions.... Thus a whole prosecution story is put into the mouth of police, witnesses for the defence though called in are not allowed to be examined by the defence counsel.... The accused is silenced if he picks up courage to say anything in defence.... Any Cantonment servant can write down the name of any citizen of the Cantonment on a chit of paper and ask him to appear the next day in court. This is a summons.... If any one does not appear in court who is thus ordered, criminal warrants of arrest are issued against him." There is much more of this style in the letter which is worth producing, but I have given enough to illustrate the writer's meaning. Let me turn for a while to this official's record during Martial Law. He is the official who tried people in batches and convicted them after a farcical trial. Witnesses have deposed to his having assembled people, having asked them to give false evidence, having removed women's veils, called them 'flies, bitches, she-asses' and having spat upon them. He it was who subjected the innocent pleaders of Shokhupura indescribable persecution. Mr. Andrews personally investigated complaints against this official and came to the conclusion that no official had behaved worse than Mr. Smith. He gathered the people of Shokhupura, humiliated them in a variety of ways, called them 'suvarlog,' 'gandi mukkhi.' His evidence before the Hunter Commission betrays his total disregard for truth and this is the officer who, if the correspondent in question has given correct facts, has been promoted. The question however is why, he is at all in Government service and why he has not been tried for assaulting and abusing innocent men and women.

I notice a desire for the impeachment of General Dyer and Sir Michael O'Dwyer. I will not stop to examine whether the course is feasible. I was sorry to find Mr. Shastriar joining this cry for the prosecution of General Dyer. If the English people will willingly do so, I would welcome such prosecution as a sign of their strong disapproval of the Jallianwalla Bagh atrocity, but I would certainly not spend a single farthing in a vain pursuit after the conviction of this man. Surely the public has received sufficient experience of the English mind. Practically the whole English Press has joined the conspiracy to screen these offenders against humanity. I would not be party to make heroes of them by joining the cry for prosecution private or public. If I can only persuade India to insist upon their complete dismissal, I should be satisfied. But more than the dismissal, of Sir Michael O'Dwyer and General Dyer, is necessary the peremptory dismissal, if not a trial, of Colonel O'Brien, Mr. Bosworth Smith, Rai Shri Ram and others mentioned in the Congress Sub-Committee's Report. Bad as General Dyer is I consider Mr. Smith to be infinitely worse and his crimes to be far more serious than the massacre of Jallianwalla Bugh. General Dyer sincerely believed that it was a soldierly act to terrorise people by shooting them. But Mr. Smith was wantonly cruel, vulgar and debased. If all the facts that have been deposed to against him are true, there is not a spark of humanity about him. Unlike General Dyer he lacks the courage to confirm what he has done and he wriggles when challenged. This officer remains free to inflict himself upon people who have done no wrong to him, and who is permitted to disgrace the rule he represents for the time being.

What is the Punjab doing? Is it not the duty of the Punjabis not to rest until they have secured the dismissal of Mr. Smith and the like? The Punjab leaders have been discharged in vain if they will not utilise the liberty they have received, in order to purge the administration of Messrs. Bosworth Smith and Company. I am sure that if they will only begin a determined agitation they will have the whole India by their side. I venture to suggest to them that the best way to qualify for sending General Dyer to the gallows is to perform the easier and the more urgent duty of arresting the mischief still continued by the officials against whom they have assisted in collecting overwhelming evidence.

GENERAL DYER

The Army Council has found General Dyer guilty of error of judgment and advised that he should not receive any office under the Crown. Mr. Montagu has been unsparing in his criticism of General Dyer's conduct. And yet somehow or other I cannot help feeling that General Dyer is by no means the worst offender. His brutality is unmistakable. His abject and unsoldier-like cowardice is apparent in every line of his amazing defence before the Army Council. He has called an unarmed crowd of men and children--mostly holiday-makers--'a rebel army.' He believes himself to be the saviour of the Punjab in that he was able to shoot down like rabbits men who were penned in an inclosure. Such a man is unworthy of being considered a soldier. There was no bravery in his action. He ran no risk. He shot without the slightest opposition and without warning. This is not an 'error of judgement.' It is paralysis of it in the face of fancied danger. It is proof of criminal incapacity and heartlessness. But the fury that has been spent upon General Dyer is, I am sure, largely misdirected. No doubt the shooting was 'frightful,' the loss of innocent life deplorable. But the slow torture, degradation and emasculation that followed was much worse, more calculated, malicious and soul-killing, and the actors who performed the deeds deserve greater condemnation that General Dyer for the Jallianwalla Bagh massacre. The latter merely destroyed a few bodies but the others tried to kill the soul of a nation. Who ever talks of Col. Frank Johnson who was by far the worst offender? He terrorised guiltless Lahore, and by his merciless orders set the tone to the whole of the Martial Law officers. But what I am concerned with is not even Col. Johnson. The first business of the people of the Punjab and of India is to rid the service of Col O'Brien, Mr. Bosworth Smith, Rai Shri Ram and Mr. Malik Khan. They are still retained in the service. Their guilt is as much proved as that of General Dyer. We shall have failed in our duty if the condemnation pronounced upon General Dyer produces a sense of satisfaction and the obvious duty of purging the administration in the Punjab is neglected. That task will not be performed by platform rhetoric or resolutions merely. Stern action is required on out part if we are to make any headway with ourselves and make any impression upon the officials that they are not to consider themselves as masters of the people but as their trusties and servants who cannot hold office if they misbehave themselves and prove unworthy of the trust reposed in them.

THE PUNJAB SENTENCES

The commissioners appointed by the Congress Punjab Sub Committee have in their report accused His Excellency the Viceroy of criminal want of imagination. His Excellency's refusal to commute two death sentences out of five is a fine illustration of the accusation. The rejection of the appeal by the Privy Council no more proves the guilt of the condemned than their innocence would have been proved by quashing the proceedings before the Martial Law Tribunal. Moreover, these cases clearly come under the Royal Proclamation in accordance with its interpretation by the Punjab Government. The murders in Amritsar were not due to any private quarrel between the murderers and their victims. The offence grave, though it was, was purely political and committed under excitement. More than full reparation has been taken for the murders and arson. In the circumstances commonsense dictates reduction of the death sentences. The popular belief favours the view that the condemned men are innocent and have not had a fair trial. The execution has been so long delayed that hanging at this stage would give a rude shock to Indian society. Any Viceroy with imagination would have at once announced commutation of the death sentences--not so Lord Chelmsford. In his estimation, evidently, the demands of justice will not be satisfied if at least some of the condemned men are not hanged. Public feeling with him counts for nothing. We shall still hope that, either the Viceroy or Mr. Montagu will commute the death sentences.

But if the Government will grievously err, if they carry out the sentences, the people will equally err if they give way to anger or grief over the hanging if it has unfortunately to take plane. Before we become a nation possessing an effective voice in the councils of nations, we must be prepared to contemplate with equanimity, not a thousand murders of innocent men and women but many thousands before we attain a status in the world that, shall not be surpassed by any nation. We hope therefore that all concerned will take rather than lose heart and treat hanging as an ordinary affair of life.

[Since the above was in type, we have received cruel news. At last H.E. the Viceroy has mercilessly given the rude shock to Indian society. It is now for the latter to take heart in spite of the unkindest cut.--Ed. Y.I.]

IV-SWARAJ

SWARAJ IN ONE YEAR

Much laughter has been indulged in at my expense for having told the Congress audience at Calcutta that if there was sufficient response to my programme of non-co-operation Swaraj would be attained in one year. Some have ignored my condition and laughed because of the impossibility of getting Swaraj anyhow within one year. Others have spelt the 'if' in capitals and suggested that if 'ifs' were permissible in argument, any absurdity could be proved to be a possibility. My proposition however is based on a mathematical calculation. And I venture to say that true Swaraj is a practical impossibility without due fulfilment of my conditions. Swaraj means a state such that we can maintain our separate existence without the presence of the English. If it is to be a partnership, it must be partnership at will. There can be no Swaraj without our feeling and being the equals of Englishmen. To-day we feel that we are dependent upon them for our internal and external security, for an armed peace between the Hindus and the Mussulmans, for our education and for the supply of daily wants, nay, even for the settlement of our religious squabbles. The Rajahs are dependent upon the British for their powers and the millionaires for their millions. The British know our helplessness and Sir Thomas Holland cracks jokes quite legitimately at the expense of non-co-operationists. To get Swaraj then is to get rid of our helplessness. The problem is no doubt stupendous even as it is for the fabled lion who having been brought up in the company of goats found it impossible to feel that he was a lion. As Tolstoy used to put it, mankind often laboured under hypnotism. Under its spell continuously we feel the feeling of helplessness. The British themselves cannot be expected to help us out of it. On the contrary, they din into our ears that we shall be fit to govern ourselves only by slow educative processes. The "Times" suggested that if we boycott the councils we shall lose the opportunity of a training in Swaraj. I have no doubt that there are many who believe what the "Times" says. It even resorts to a falsehood. It audaciously says that Lord Milner's Mission listened to the Egyptians only when they were ready to lift the boycott of the Egyptian Council. For me the only training in Swaraj we need is the ability to defend ourselves against the whole world and to live our natural life in perfect freedom even though it may be full of defects. Good Government is no substitute for self-Government. The Afghans have a bad Government but it is self-Government. I envy them. The Japanese learnt the art through a sea of blood. And if we to-day had the power to drive out the English by superior brute force, we would be counted their superiors, and in spite of our inexperience in debating at the Council table or in holding executive offices, we would be held fit to govern ourselves. For brute force is the only test the west has hitherto recognised. The Germans were defeated not because they were necessarily in the wrong, but because the allied Powers were found to possess greater brute strength. In the end therefore India must either learn the art of war which the British will not teach her or, she must follow her own way of discipline and self-sacrifice through non-co-operation. It is as amazing as it is humiliating that less than one hundred-thousand white men should be able to rule three hundred and fifteen million Indians. They do so somewhat undoubtedly by force, but more by securing our co-operation in a thousand ways and making us more and more helpless and dependent on them as time goes forward. Let us not mistake reformed councils, more lawcourts and even governorships for real freedom or power. They are but subtler methods of emasculation. The British cannot rule us by mere force. And so they resort to all means, honourable and dishonourable, in order to retain their hold on India. They want India's billions and they want India's man power for their imperialistic greed. If we refuse to supply them with men and money, we achieve our goal, namely, Swaraj, equality, manliness.

The cup of our humiliation was filled during the closing scenes in the Viceregal Council. Mr. Shustri could not move his resolution on the Punjab. The Indian victims of Jullianwala received Rs. 1,250, the English victims of mob-frenzy received lakhs. The officials who were guilty of crimes against those whose servants they were, were reprimanded. And the councillors were satisfied. If India were powerful, India would not have stood this addition of insult, to her injury.

I do not blame the British. If we were weak in numbers as they are, we too would perhaps have resorted to the same methods as they are now employing. Terrorism and deception are weapons not of the strong but of the weak. The British are weak in numbers we are weak in spite of our numbers. The result is that each is dragging the other down. It is common experience that Englishmen lose in character after residence in India and that Indians lose in courage and manliness by contact with Englishmen. This process of weakening is good neither for us, two nations, nor for the world.

But if we Indians take care of ourselves the English and the rest of the world would take care of themselves. Our contributions to the world's progress must therefore consist in setting our own house in order.

Training in arms for the present is out of the question. I go a step further and believe that India has a better mission for the world. It is within her to show that she can achieve her destiny by pure self-sacrifice, i.e., self-purification. This can be done only by non-co-operation. And non-co-operation is possible only when those who commenced to co-operate being the process of withdrawal. If we can but free ourselves from the threefold *maya* of Government-controlled schools, Government law-courts and legislative councils, and truly control our own education regulate our disputes and be indifferent to their legislation, we are ready to govern ourselves and we are only then ready to ask the government servants, whether civil or military, to resign, and the tax-payers to suspend payment of taxes.

And is it such an impracticable proposition to expect parents to withdraw their children from schools and colleges and establish their own institutions or to ask lawyers to suspend their practice and devote their whole time attention to national service against payment where necessary, of their maintenance, or to ask candidates for councils not to enter councils and lend their passive or active assistance to the legislative machinery through which all control is exercised. The movement of non-co-operation is nothing but an attempt to isolate the brute force of the British from all the trappings under which it is hidden and to show that brute force by itself cannot for one single moment hold India.

But I frankly confess that, until the three conditions mentioned by me are fulfilled, there is no Swaraj. We may not go on taking our college degrees, taking thousands of rupees monthly from clients for cases which can be finished in five minutes and taking the keenest delight in wasting national time on the council floor and still expect to gain national self-respect.

The last though not the least important part of the Maya still remains to be considered. That is Swadeshi. Had we not abandoned Swadeshi, we need not have been in the present fallen state. If we would get rid of the economic slavery, we must manufacture our own cloth and at the present moment only by hand-spinning and hand weaving.

All this means discipline, self-denial, self-sacrifice, organising ability, confidence and courage. If we show this in one year among the classes that to-day count, and make public opinion, we certainly gain Swaraj within one year. If I am told that even we who lead have not these qualities in us, there certainly will never be Swaraj for India, but then we shall have no right to blame the English for what they are doing. Our salvation and its time are solely dependent upon us.

BRITISH RULE--AN EVIL

The

Interpreter

is however more to the point in asking, "Does Mr. Gandhi hold without hesitation or reserve that British rule in India is altogether an evil and that the people of India are to be taught so to regard it? He must hold it to be so evil that the wrongs it does outweigh the benefit it confers, for only so is non-co-operation to be justified at the bar of conscience or of Christ." My answer is emphatically in the affirmative. So long as I believed that the sum total of the energy of the British Empire was good, I clung to it despite what I used to regard as temporary aberrations. I am not sorry for having done so. But having my eyes opened, it would be sin for me to associate myself with the Empire unless it purges itself of its evil character. I write this with sorrow and I should be pleased if I discovered that I was in error and that my present attitude was a reaction. The continuous financial drain, the emasculation of the Punjab and the betrayal of the Muslim sentiment constitute, in my humble opinion, a threefold robbery of India. 'The blessings of

pax Britanica

' I reckon, therefore, to be a curse. We would have at least remained like the other nations brave men and women, instead of feeling as we do so utterly helpless, if we had no British Rule imposing on us an armed peace. 'The blessing' of roads and railways is a return no self-respecting nation would accept for its degradation. 'The blessing' of education is proving one of the greatest obstacles in our progress towards freedom.

A MOVEMENT OF PURIFICATION

The fact is that non-co-operation by reason of its non-violence has become a religious and purifying movement. It is daily bringing strength to the nation, showing it its weak spots and the remedy for removing them. It is a movement of self-reliance. It is the mightiest force for revolutionising opinion and stimulating thought. It is a movement of self-imposed suffering and therefore possesses automatic checks against extravagance or impatience. The capacity of the nation for suffering regulates its advance towards freedom. It isolates the force of evil by refraining from participation in it, in any shape or form.

WHY WAS INDIA LOST?

[A dialog between the Reader and Editor,--

Indian Home Rule].

Reader: You have said much about civilisation--enough to make me ponder over it. I do not know what I should adopt and what I should avoid from the nations of Europe. but one question comes to my lips immediately. If civilisation is a disease, and if it has attacked England why has she been able to take India, and why is she able to retain it?

Editor: Your question is not very difficult to answer, and we shall presently be able to examine the true nature of Swaraj; for I am aware that I have still to answer that question. I will, however, take up your previous question. The English have not taken India; we have given it to them. They are not in India because of their strength, but because we keep them. Let us now see whether these positions can be sustained. They came to our country originally for the purpose of trade. Recall the Company Bahadur. Who made it Bahadur? They had not the slightest intention at the time of establishing a kingdom. Who assisted the Company's officers? Who was tempted at the sight of their silver? Who bought their goods? History testifies that we did all this. In order to become rich all at once, we welcomed the Company's officers with open arms. We assisted them. If I am in the habit of drinking Bhang, and a seller thereof sells it to me, am I to blame him or myself? By blaming the seller shall I be able to avoid the habit? And, if a particular retailer is driven away will not another take his place? A true servant of India will have to go to the root of the matter. If an excess of food has caused me indigestion I will certainly not avoid it by blaming water. He is a true physician who probes the cause of disease and, if you pose as a physician for the disease of India, you will have to find out its true cause.

Reader: You are right. Now, I think you will not have to argue much with me to drive your conclusions home. I am impatient to know your further views. We are now on a most interesting topic. I shall, therefore, endeavour to follow your thought, and stop you when I am in doubt.

Editor: I am afraid that, in spite of your enthusiasm, as we proceed further we shall have differences of opinion. Nevertheless, I shall argue only when you will stop me. We have already seen that the English merchants were able to get a footing in India because we encouraged them. When our princes fought among themselves, they sought the assistance of Company Bahadar. That corporation was versed alike in commerce and war. It was unhampered by questions of morality. Its object was to increase its commerce and to make money. It accepted our assistance, and increased the number of its warehouses. To protect the latter it employed an army which was utilised by us also. Is it not then useless to blame the English for what we did at that time? The Hindus and the Mahomedans were at daggers drawn. This, too, gave the Company its opportunity, and thus we created the circumstances that gave the Company its control over India. Hence it is truer to say that we gave India to the English than that India was lost.

Reader: Will you now tell me how they are able to retain India?

Editor: The causes that gave them India enable them to retain it. Some Englishmen state that they took, and they hold, India by the sword. Both these statements are wrong. The sword is entirely useless for holding India. We alone keep them. Napoleon is said to have described the English as a nation of shop keepers. It is a fitting description. They hold whatever dominions they have for the sake of their commerce. Their army and their navy are intended to protect it. When the Transvaal offered no such attractions, the late Mr. Gladstone discovered that it was no right for the English to hold it. When it became a paying proposition, resistance led to war. Mr. Chamberlain soon discovered that England enjoyed a suzerainty over the Transvaal. It is related that some one asked the late President Kruger whether there was gold in the moon? He replied that it was highly unlikely, because, if there were, the English would have annexed it. Many problems can be solved by remembering that money is their God. Then it follows that we keep the English in India for our base self-interest. We like their commerce, they please us by their subtle methods, and get what they want from us. To blame them for this is to perpetuate their power. We further strengthen their hold by quarrelling amongst ourselves. If you accept the above statements, it is proved that the English entered India for the purposes of trade. They remain in it for the same purpose, and we help them to do so. Their arms and ammunition are perfectly useless. In this connection, I remind you that it is the British flag which is waving in Japan, and not the Japanese. The English have a treaty with Japan for the sake of their commerce and you will see that, if they can manage it, their commerce will greatly expand in that country. They wish to convert the whole word into a vast market for their goods. That they cannot do so is true, but the blame will not be theirs. They will leave no stone unturned to reach the goal.

SWARAJ MY IDEAL

The following is a fairly full report of Mr. Gandhi's important speech at Calcutta on the 13th December 1920:--

The very fact, that so many of you cannot understand Hindi which is bound to be the National medium of expression throughout Hindustan in gatherings of Indians belonging to different parts of the land, shows the depth of the degradation to which we have sunk, and points to the supreme necessity of the non-co-operation movement which is intended to lift us out of that condition. This Government has been instrumental in degrading this great nation in various ways, and it is impossible to be free from it without co-operation amongst ourselves which is in turn impossible without a national medium of expression.

But I am not here to day to plead for the medium. I am to plead for the acceptance by the country of the programme of non-violent, progressive non-co-operation. Now all the words that I have used here are absolutely necessary and the two adjectives 'progressive' and 'non-violent' are integral part of a whole. With me non-violence is part of my religion, a matter of creed. But with the great number of Mussalmans non-violence is a policy, with thousand, if not millions of Hindus, it is equally a matter of policy. But whether it is a creed or a policy, it is utterly impossible for you to finish the programme for the enfranchisement of the millions of India, without recognising the necessity and the value of non-violence. Violence may for a moment avail to secure a certain measure of success but it could not in the long run achieve any appreciable result. On the other hand all violence would prove destructive to the honour and self-respect of the nation. The blue books issued by the Government of India show that inasmuch as we have used violence, military expenditure has gone up, not proportionately but in geometrical progression. The bonds of our slavery have been forged all the stronger for our having offered violence. And the whole history of British rule in India is a demonstration of the fact that we have never been able to offer successful violence. Whilst therefore I say that rather than have the yoke of a Government that has so emasculated us, I would welcome violence. I would urge with all the emphasis that I can command that India will never be able to regain her own by methods of violence.

Lord Ronaldshay who has done me the honour of reading my booklet on Home Rule has warned my countrymen against engaging themselves in a struggle for a Swaraj such as is described in that booklet. Now though I do not want to withdraw a single word of it, I would say to you on this occasion that I do not ask India to follow out to-day the methods prescribed in my booklet. If they could do that they would have Home Rule not in a year but in a day, and India by realising that ideal wants to acquire an ascendancy over the rest of the world. But it must remain a day dream more or less for the time being. What I am doing to-day is that I am giving the country a pardonable programme not the abolition of law courts, posts, telegraphs and of railways but for the attainment of Parliamentary Swarja. I am telling you to do that so long as we do not isolate ourselves from this Government, we are co-operating with it through schools, law courts and councils, through service civil and military and payment of taxes and foreign trade.

The moment this fact is realised and non-co-operation is effected, this Government must totter to pieces. If I know that the masses were prepared for the whole programme at once, I would not delay in putting it at once to work. It is not possible at the present moment, to prevent the masses from bursting out into wrath against those who come to execute the law, it is not possible, that the military would lay down their arms without the slightest violence. If that were possible to-day, I would propose all the stages of non-co-operation to be worked simultaneously. But we have not secured that control over the masses, we have uselessly frittered away precious years of the nation's life in mastering a language which we need least for winning our liberty; we have frittered away all those years in learning liberty from Milton and Shakespeare, in deriving inspiration from the pages of Mill, whilst liberty could be learnt at our doors. We have thus succeeded in isolating ourselves from the masses: we have been westernised. We have failed these 35 years to utilise our education in order to permeate the masses. We have sat upon the pedestal and from there delivered harangues to them in a language they do not understand and we see to-day that we are unable to conduct large gatherings in a disciplined manner. And discipline is the essence of success. Here is therefore one reason why I have introduced the word 'progressive' in the non-co-operation Resolution. Without any impertinence I may say that I understand the mass mind better than any one amongst the educated Indians. I contend that the masses are not ready for suspension of payment of taxes. They have not yet learnt sufficient self-control. If I was sure of non-violence on their part I would ask them to suspend payment to-day and not waste a single moment of the nations time. With me the liberty of India has become a passion. Liberty of Islam is as dear to me. I would not therefore delay a moment if I found that the whole of the programme could be enforced at once.

It grieves me to miss the faces of dear and revered leaders in this assembly. We miss here the trumpet voice of Surendranath Banorji, who has rendered inestimable service to the country. And though we stand as poles asunder to-day, though we may have sharp differences with him, we must express them with becoming restraint. I do not ask you to give up a single iota of principle. I urge non-violence in language and in deed. If non-violence is essential in our dealings with Government, it is more essential in our dealings with our leaders. And it grieves me deeply to hear of recent instances of violence reported to have been used in East Bongal against our own people. I was pained to hear that the ears of a man who had voted at the recent elections had been cut, and night soil had been thrown into the bed of a man who had stood as a candidate. Non-co-operation is never going to succeed in this way. It will not succeed unless we create an atmosphere of perfect freedom, unless we prize our opponents liberty as much as our own. The liberty of faith, conscience, thought and action which we claim for ourselves must be conceded equally to others. Non co-operation is a process of purification and we must continually try to touch the hearts of those who differ from us, their minds, and their emotions, but never their bodies. Discipline and restraint are the cardinal principles of our conduct and I warn you against any sort of tyrannical social ostracism. I was deeply grieved therefore to hear of the insult offered to a dead body in Delhi and feel that if it was the action of non-co-operators they have disgraced themselves and their creed. I repeat we cannot deliver our land through violence.

It was not a joke when I said on the congress platform that Swaraj could be established in one year if there was sufficient response from the nation. Three months of this year are gone. If we are true to our salt, true to our nation, true to the songs we sing, if we are true to the Bhagwad Gita and the Koran, we would finish the programme in the remaining nine months and deliver Islam the Punjab and India.

I have proposed a limited programme workable within one year, having a special regard to the educated classes. We seem to be labouring under the illusion that we cannot possibly live without Councils, law courts and schools provided by the Government. The moment we are disillusioned we have Swaraj. It is demoralising both for Government and the governed that a hundred thousand pilgrims should dictate terms to a nation composed of three hundred millions. And how is it they can thus dictate terms. It is because we have been divided and they have ruled. I have never forgotten Humes' frank confession that the British Government was sustained by the policy of "Divide and Rule." Therefore it is that I have laid stress upon Hindu Muslim Unity as one of the important essentials for the success of Non-co-operation. But, it should be no lip unity, nor bunia unity it should be a unity broad based on a recognition of the heart. If we want to save Hinduism, I say for Gods sake, do not seek to bargain with the

Mussalmans. I have been going about with Maulana Shaukat Ali all these months, but I have not so much as whispered anything about the protection of the cow. My alliance with the Ali Brothers is one of honour. I feel that I am on my honour, the whole of Hinduism is on its honour, and if it will not be found wanting, it will do its duty towards the Mussalmans of India. Any bargaining would be degrading to us. Light brings light not darkness, and nobility done with a noble purpose will be twice rewarded. It will be God alone who can protect the cow. Ask me not to-day--'what about the cow,' ask me after Islam is vindicated through India. Ask the Rajas what they do to entertain their English guests. Do they not provide beef and champagne for their guests. Persuade them first to stop cow killing and then think of bargaining with Mussalmans. And how are we Hindus behaving ourselves towards the cow and her progeny! Do we treat her as our religion requires us? Not till we have set our own house in order and saved the cow from the Englishmen have we the right to plead on her behalf with the Mussalmans. And the best way of saving the cow from them is to give them unconditional help in their hour of trouble.

Similarly what do we owe the Punjab? The whole of India was made to crawl on her belly in as much as a single Punjabi was made to crawl in that dirty lane in Amritsar, the whole womanhood of India was unveiled in as much as the innocent woman of Manianwalla were unveiled by an insolent office; and Indian childhood was dishonoured in that, that school children of tender age were made to walk four times a day to stated places within the martial area in the Punjab and to salute the Union Jack, through the effect of which order two children, seven years old died of sunstroke having been made to wait in the noonday sun. In my opinion it is a sin to attend the schools and colleges conducted under the aegis of this Government so long as it has not purged itself of these crimes by proper repentance. We may not with any sense of self-respect plead before the courts of the Government when we remember that it was through the Punjab Courts that innocent men were sentenced to be imprisoned and hanged. We become participators in the crime of the Government by voluntarily helping it or being helped by it.

The women of India have intuitively understood the spiritual nature of the struggle. Thousands have attended to listen to the message of non-violent non-co-operation and have given me their precious ornaments for the purpose of advancing the cause of Swaraj. Is it any wonder if I believe the possibility of gaining Swaraj within a year after all these wonderful demonstrations? I would be guilty of want of faith in God if I under-rated the significance of the response from the women of India. I hope that the students will do their duty. The country certainly expects the lawyers who have hitherto led public agitation to recognise the new awakening.

I have used strong language but I have done so with the greatest deliberation, I am not actuated by any feeling of revenge. I do not consider Englishmen as my enemy. I recognise the worth of many. I enjoy the privilege of having many English friends, but I am a determined enemy of the English rule as is conducted at present and if the power--tapasya--of one man could destroy it, I would certainly destroy it, if it could not be mended. An Empire that stands for injustice and breach of faith does not deserve to stand if its custodians will not repent and non-co-operation has been devised in order to enable the nation to compel justice.

I hope that Bengal will take her proper place in this movement of self-purification. Bengal began Swadeshi and national education when the rest of India was sleeping. I hope that Bengal will come to the front in this movement for gaining Swaraj and gaining justice for the Khilafat and the Punjab through purification and self-sacrifice.

ON THE WRONG TRACK

Lord Ronaldshay has been doing me the favour of reading my booklet on Indian Home Rule which is a translation of Hind Swaraj. His Lordship told his audience that if Swaraj meant what I had described it to be in the booklet, the Bengalis would have none of it. I am sorry that Swaraj of the Congress resolution does not mean the Swaraj depicted in the booklet; Swaraj according to the Congress means Swaraj that the people of India want, not what the British Government may condescend to give. In so far as I can see, Swaraj will be a Parliament chosen by the people with the fullest power over the finance, the police, the military, the navy, the courts, and the educational institutions.

I am free to confess that the Swaraj I expect to gain within one year, if India responds will be such Swaraj as will make practically impossible the repetition of the Khilafat and the Punjab wrongs, and will enable the nation to do good or evil as it chooses, and not he 'good' at the dictation of an irresponsible, insolent, and godless bureaucracy. Under that Swaraj the nation will have the power to impose a heavy protective tariff on such foreign goods as are capable of being manufactured in India, as also the power to refuse to send a single soldier outside India for the purpose of enslaving the surrounding or remote nationalities. The Swaraj that I dream of will be a possibility only, when the nation is free to make its choice both of good and evil.

I adhere to all I have said in that booklet and I would certainly recommend it to the reader. Government over self is the truest Swaraj, it is synonymous with

moksha

or salvation, and I have seen nothing to alter the view that doctors, lawyers, and railways are no help, and are often a hindrance, to the one thing worth striving after. But I know that association, a satanic activity, such as the Government is engaged in, makes even an effort for such freedom a practical impossibility. I cannot tender allegiance to God and Satan at the same time.

The surest sign of the satanic nature of the present system is that even a nobleman of the type of Lord Ronaldshay is obliged to put us off the track. He will not deal with the one thing needful. Why is he silent about the Punjab? Why does he evade the Khilafat? Can ointments soothe a patient who is suffering from corroding consumption? Does his lordship not see that it is not the inadequacy of the reforms that has set India aflame but that it is the infliction of the two wrongs and the wicked attempt to make us forget them? Does he not see that a complete change of heart is required before reconciliation?

But it has become the fashion nowadays to ascribe hatred to non-co-operationism. And I regret to find that even Col. Wedgewood has fallen into the trap. I make bold to say that the only way to remove hatred is to give it disciplined vent. No man can--I cannot--perform the impossible task of removing hatred so long as contempt and despise for the feelings of India are sedulously nursed. It is a mockery to ask India not to hate when in the same breath India's most sacred feelings are contemptuously brushed aside. India feels weak and helpless and so expresses her helplessness by hating the tyrant who despises her and makes her crawl on the belly, lifts the veils of her innocent women and compels her tender children to acknowledge his power by saluting his flag four times a day. The gospel of Non-co-operation addresses itself to the task of making the people strong and self-reliant. It is an attempt to transform hatred into pity. A strong and self-reliant India will cease to hate Bosworth Smiths and Frank Johnsons, for she will have the power to punish them and therefore the power also to pity and forgive them. To-day she can neither punish nor forgive, and therefore helplessly nurses hatred. If the Mussalmans were strong, they would not hate the English but would fight and wrest from them the dearest possessions of Islam. I know that the Ali Brothers who live only for the honour and the prestige of Islam, and are prepared any moment to die for it, will to-day make friends with the latter Englishmen, if they were to do justice to the Khilafat which it is in their power to do.

I am positively certain that there is no personal element in this fight. Both the Hindus and the Mahomedans would to-day invoke blessings on the English if they would but give proof positive of their goodness, faithfulness, and loyalty to India. Non-co-operation then is a godsend; it will purify and strengthen India; and a strong India will be a strength to the world as an Indian weak and helpless is a curse to mankind. Indian soldiers have involuntarily helped to destroy Turkey and are now destroying the flower of the Arabian nation. I cannot recall a single campaign in which the Indian soldier has been employed by the British Government for the good of mankind. And yet, (Oh! the shame of it!) Indian Maharajas are never tired of priding themselves on the loyal help they have rendered the English! Could degradation sink any lower?

THE CONGRESS CONSTITUTION

The belated report of the Congress Constitution Committee has now been published for general information and opinion has been invited from all public bodies in order to assist the deliberations of the All India Congress Committee. It is a pity that, small though the Constitution Committee was, all the members never met at any one time in spite of efforts, to have a meeting of them all. It is perhaps no body's fault that all the members could not meet. At the same time the draft report has passed through the searching examination of all but one member and the report represents the mature deliberations of four out of the five members. It must be stated at the same time that it does not pretend to be the unanimous opinion of the members. Rather than present a dissenting minute, a workable scheme has been brought out leaving each member free to press his own views on the several matters in which they are not quite unanimous. The most important part of the constitution, however, is the alteration of the creed. So far as I am aware there is no fundamental difference of opinion between the members.

In my opinion the altered creed represents the exact feeling of the country at the present moment.

I know that the proposed alteration has been subjected to hostile criticism in several newspapers of note. But the extraordinary situation that faces the country is that popular opinion is far in advance of several newspapers which have hitherto commanded influence and have undoubtedly moulded public opinion. The fact is that the formation of opinion to-day is by no means confined to the educated classes, but the masses have taken it upon themselves not only to formulate opinion but to enforce it. It would be a mistake to belittle or ignore this opinion, or to ascribe it to a temporary upheaval. It would be equally a mistake to suppose that this awakening amongst the masses is due either to the activity of the Ali Brothers or myself. For the time being we have the ear of the masses because we voice their sentiments. The masses are by no means so foolish or unintelligent as we sometimes imagine. They often perceive things with their intuition, which we ourselves fail to see with our intellect. But whilst the masses know what they want, they often do not know how to express their wants and, less often, how to get what they want. Herein comes the use of leadership, and disastrous results can easily follow a bad, hasty, or what is worse, selfish lead.

The first part of the proposed creed expresses the present desire of the nation, and the second shows the way that desire can be fulfilled. In my humble opinion the Congress creed with the proposed alteration is but an extension of the original. And so long as no break with the British connection is attempted, it is strictly within even the existing article that defines the Congress creed. The extension lies in the contemplated possibility of a break with the British connection. In my humble opinion, if India is to make unhampered progress, we must make it clear to the British people that whilst we desire to retain the British connection, if we can rise to our full height with it we are determined to dispense with, and even to get rid of that connection, if that is necessary for full national development. I hold that it is not only derogatory to national dignity but it actually impedes national progress superstitiously to believe that our progress towards our goal is impossible without British connection. It is this superstition which makes some of the best of us tolerate the Punjab wrong and the Khilafat insult. This blind adherence to that connection makes us feel helpless. The proposed alteration in the creed enables us to rid ourselves of our helpless condition. I personally hold that it is perfectly constitutional openly to strive after independence, but lest there may be dispute as to the constitutional character of any movement for complete independence, the doubtful and highly technical adjective "constitutional" has been removed from the altered creed in the draft. Surely it should be enough to ensure that the methods for achieving our end are legitimate, honourable, and peaceful, I believe that this was the reasoning that guided my colleagues in accepting the proposed creed. In any case, such was certainly my view of the whole alteration. There is no desire on my part to adopt any means that are subversive of law and order. I know, however, that I am treading on delicate ground when I write about law and order for, to some of our distinguished leaders even my present methods appear to be lawless and conducive to disorder. But even they will perhaps grant that the retention of the word 'constitutional' cannot protect the country against methods such as I am employing. It gives rise, no doubt, to a luminous legal discussion, but any such discussion is fruitless when the nation means business. The other important alteration refers to the limitation of the number of delegates. I believe that the advantages of such a limitation are obvious. We are fast reaching a time when without any such limitation the Congress will become an unwieldy body. It is difficult even to have an unlimited number of visitors; it is impossible to transact national business if we have an unlimited number of delegates.

The next important alteration is about the election of the members of the All-India Congress Committee, making that committee practically the Subjects Committee, and the redistribution of India for the purposes of the Congress on a linguistic basis. It is not necessary to comment on these alterations, but I wish to add that if the Congress accepts the principle of limiting the number of delegates it would be advisable to introduce the principle of proportional representation. That would enable all parties who wish to be represented at the Congress.

I observe that *the Servant of India* sees an inconsistency between my implied acceptance of the British Committee, so far as the published draft constitution is concerned, and my recent article in *Young India* on that Committee and the newspaper *India*. But it is well known that for several years I have held my present views about the existence of that body. It would have been irrelevant for me, perhaps, to suggest to my colleagues the extinction of that committee. It was not our function to report on the usefulness or otherwise of the Committee. We were commissioned only for preparing a new constitution. Moreover I knew that my colleagues were not averse to the existence of the British Committee. And the drawing up of a new constitution enabled me to show that where there was no question of principle I was desirous of agreeing quickly with my opponents in opinions.

But I propose certainly to press for abolition of the committee as it is at present continued, and the stopping of its organ *India*.

SWARAJ IN NINE MONTHS

Asked by the

Times

representative as to his impressions formed as a result of his activities during the last three months, Mr. Gandhi said:--"My own impression of these three months' extensive experience is that this movement of non-co-operation has come to stay, and it is most decidedly a purifying movement, in spite of isolated instances of rowdyism, as for instance at Mrs. Besant's meeting in Bombay, at some places in Delhi, Bengal, and even in Gujarat. The people are assimilating day after day the spirit of non-violence, not necessarily as a creed, but as an inevitable policy. I expect most startling results, more startling than, say, the discoveries of Sir J.C. Bose, or the acceptance by the people of non-violence. If the Government could be assured beyond any possibility of doubt that no violence would ever be offered by us the Government would from that moment alter its character, unconsciously and involuntarily, but nonetheless surely on that account."

"Alter its character,--in what, direction?" asked the *Times* representative.

"Certainly in the direction which we ask it should move--that being in the direction of Government becoming responsive to every call of the nation."

"Will you kindly explain further?" asked the representative.

"By that I mean," said Mr. Gandhi, "people will be able by asserting themselves through fixed determination and self-sacrifice to gain the redress of the Khilafat wrong, the Punjab wrong, and attain the Swaraj of their choice."

"But what is your Swaraj, and where does the Government come in there--the Government which, you say will alter its character unconsciously?"

"My Swaraj," said Mr. Gandhi, "is the Parliamentary Government of India in the modern sense of the term for the time being, and that Government would be secured to us either through the friendly offices of the British people or without them."

"What do you mean by the phrase, 'without them!'" questioned the interviewer.

"This movement," continued Mr. Gandhi, "is an endeavour to purge the present Government of selfishness and greed which determine almost every one of their activities. Suppose that we have made it impossible by disassociation from them to feed their greed. They might not wish to remain in India, as happened in the case of Somaliland, where the moment its administration ceased to be a paying proposition they evacuated it."

"How do you think," queried the representative, "in practice this will work out?"

"What I have sketched before you," said Mr. Gandhi, "is the final possibility. What I expect is that nothing of that kind will happen. In so far as I understand the British people I will recognise the force of public opinion when it has become real and patent. Then, and only then, will they realise the hideous injustice which in their name the Imperial ministers and their representatives in India have perpetrated. They will therefore remedy the two wrongs in accordance with the wishes of the people, and they will also offer a constitution exactly in accordance with the wishes of the people of India, as represented by their chosen leaders.

"Supposing that the British Government wish to retire because India is not a paying concern, what do you think will then be the position of India?"

Mr. Gandhi answered: "At that stage surely it is easy to understand that India will then have evolved either outstanding spiritual height or the ability to offer violence, against violence. She will have evolved an organising ability of a high order, and will therefore be in every way able to cope with any emergency that might arise." "In other words," observed the *Times* representative, "you expect the moment of the British evacuation, if such a contingency arises, will coincide with the moment of India's preparedness and ability and conditions favourable for India to take over the Indian administration as a going concern and work it for the benefit and advancement of the Nation?"

Mr. Gandhi answered the question with an emphatic affirmative. "My experience during the last months fills me with the hope," continued Mr. Gandhi, "that within the nine months that remain of the year in which I have expected Swaraj for India we shall redress the two wrongs and we shall see Swaraj established in accordance with the wishes of the people of India."

"Where will the present Government be at the end of the nine months?" Asked the *Times* representative.

Mr. Gandhi, with a significant smile, said: "The lion will then lie with the lamb."

Young India, December, 1920.

THE ATTAINMENT OF SWARAJ

Mr. Gandhi in moving his resolution on the creed before the Congress, said, "The resolution which I have the honour to move is as follows: The object of the Indian National Congress is the attainment of Swarajya by the people of India by all legitimate and peaceful means."

There are only two kinds of objections, so far as I understand, that will be advanced from this platform. One is that we may not to-day think of dissolving the British connection. What I say is that it is derogatory to national dignity to think of permanence of British connection at any cost. We are labouring under a grievous wrong, which it is the personal duty of every Indian to get redressed. This British Government not only refused to redress the wrong, but it refuses to acknowledge *its* mistake and so long as it retains its attitude, it is not possible for us to say all that we want to be or all that we want to get, retaining British connection. No matter what difficulties be in our path, we must make the clearest possible declaration to the world and to the whole of India, that we may not possibly have British connection, if the British people will not do this elementary justice. I do not, for one moment, suggest that we want to end at the British connection at all costs, unconditionally. If the British connection is for the advancement of India, we do not want to destroy it. But if it is inconsistent with our national self respect, then it is our bounden duty to destroy it. There is room in this resolution for both--those who believe that, by retaining British connection, we can purify ourselves and purify British people, and those who have no belief. As for instance, take the extreme case of Mr. Andrews. He says all hope for India is gone for keeping the British connection. He says there must be complete severance--complete independence. There is room enough in this creed for a man like Mr. Andrews also. Take another illustration, a man like myself or my brother Shaukat Ali. There is certainly no room for us, if we have eternally to subscribe to the doctrine, whether these wrongs are redressed or not, we shall have to evolve ourselves within the British Empire; there is no room for me in that creed. Therefore this creed is elastic enough to take in both shades of opinions and the British people will have to beware that, if they do not want to do justice, it will be the bounden duty of every Indian to destroy the Empire.

I want just now to wind up my remarks with a personal appeal, drawing your attention to an object lesson that was presented in the Bengal camp yesterday. If you want Swaraj, you have got a demonstration of how to get Swaraj. There was a little bit of skirmish, a little bit of squabble, and a little bit of difference in the Bengal camp, as there will always be differences so long as the world lasts. I have known differences between husband and wife, because I am still a husband; I have noticed differences between parents and children, because I am still a father of four boys, and they are all strong enough to destroy their father so far as bodily struggle is concerned; I possess that varied experience of husband and parent; I know that we shall always have squabbles, we shall always have differences but the lesson that I want to draw your attention to is that I had the honour and privilege of addressing both the parties. They gave me their undivided attention and what is more they showed their attachment, their affection and their fellowship for me by accepting the humble advice that I had the honour of tendering to them, and I told them I am not here to distribute justice that can be awarded only through our worthy president. But I ask you not to go to the president, you need not worry him. If you are strong, if you are brave, if you are intent upon getting Swaraj, and if you really want to revise the creed, then you will bottle up your rage, you will bottle up all the feelings of injustice that may rankle in your hearts and forget these things here under this very roof and I told them to forget their differences, to forgot the wrongs. I don't want to tell you or go into the history of that incident. Probably most of you know. I simply want to invite your attention to the fact. I don't say they have settled up their differences. I hope they have but I do know that they undertook to forget the differences. They undertook not to worry the President, they undertook not to make any demonstration here or in the Subjects Committee. All honour to those who listened to that advice.

I only wanted my Bengali friends and all the other friends who have come to this great assembly with a fixed determination to seek nothing but the settlement of their country, to seek nothing but the advancement of their respective rights, to seek nothing but the conservation of the national honour. I appeal to every one of you to copy the example set by those who felt aggrieved and who felt that their heads were broken. I know, before we have done with this great battle on which we have embarked at the special sessions of the Congress, we have to go probably, possibly through a sea of blood, but let it not be said of us or any one of us that we are guilty of shedding blood, but let it be said by generations yet to be born that we suffered, that we shed not somebody's blood but our own, and so I have no hesitation in saying that I do not want to show much sympathy for those who had their heads broken or who were said to be even in danger of losing their lives. What does it matter? It is much better to die at the hands, at least, of our own countrymen. What is there to revenge ourselves about or upon. So I ask everyone of you that if at any time there is blood-boiling within you against some fellow countrymen of yours, even though he may be in the employ of Government, though he may be in the Secret Service, you will take care not to be offended and not to return blow for blow. Understand that the very moment you return the blow from the detective, your cause is lost. This is your non-violent campaign. And so I ask everyone of you not to retaliate but to bottle up all your rage, to dismiss your rage from you and you will rise graver men. I am here to congratulate those who have restrained themselves from going to the President and bringing the dispute before him.

Therefore I appeal to those who feel aggrieved to feel that they have done the right thing in forgetting it and if they have not forgotten I ask them to try to forget the thing; and that is the object lesson to which I wanted to draw your attention if you want to carry this resolution. Do not carry this resolution only by an acclamation for this resolution, but I want you to accompany the carrying out of this resolution with a faith and resolve which nothing on earth can move. That you are intent upon getting Swaraj at the earliest possible moment and that you are intent upon getting Swaraj by means that are legitimate, that are honourable and by means that are non-violent, that are peaceful, you have resolved upon, so far you can say to-day. We cannot give battle to this Government by means of steel, but we can give battle by exercising, what I have so often called, "soul force" and soul force is not the prerogative of one man of a Sanyasi or even a so-called saint. Soul force is the prerogative of every human being, female or male and therefore I ask my countrymen, if they want to accept this resolution, to accept it with that firm determination and to understand that it is inaugurated under such good and favourable auspices as I have described to you.

In my humble opinion, the Congress will have done the rightest thing, if it unanimously adopts this resolution. May God grant that you will pass this resolution unanimously, may God grant that you will also have the courage and the ability to carry out the resolution and that within one year.

V-HINDU MOSLEM UNITY

[A dialogue between Editor and reader on the Hindu-Moslem Unity--*Indian Home Rule*.]

THE HINDUS AND THE MAHOMEDANS.

EDITOR: Your last question is a serious one, and yet, on careful consideration, it will be found to be easy of solution. The question arises because of the presence of the railways of the lawyers, and of the doctors. We shall presently examine the last two. We have already considered the railways. I should, however, like to add that man is so made by nature as to require him to restrict his movements as far as his hands and feet will take him. If we did not rush about from place to place by means of railways such other maddening conveniences, much of the confusion that arises would be obviated. Our difficulties are of our own creation. God set a limit to a man's locomotive ambition in the construction of his body. Man immediately proceeded to discover means of overriding the limit. God gifted man with intellect that he might know his Maker. Man abused it, so that he might forget his Maker. I am so constructed that I can only serve my immediate neighbours, but, in my conceit, I pretend to have discovered that I must with my body serve every individual in the Universe. In thus attempting the impossible, man comes in contact with different natures, different religions, and is utterly confounded. According to this reasoning, it must be apparent to you that railways are a most dangerous institution. Man has therefore gone further away from his Maker.

READER: But I am impatient to hear your answer to my question. Has the introduction of Mahomedanism not unmade the nation?

EDITOR: India cannot cease to be one nation because people belonging to different religions live in it. The introduction of foreigners does not necessarily destroy the nation, they merge in it. A country is one nation only when such a condition obtains in it. That country must have a faculty for assimilation. India has ever been such a country. In reality, there are as many religions as there are individuals, but those who are conscious of the spirit of nationality do not interfere with one another's religion. If they do, they are not fit to be considered a nation. If the Hindus believe that India should be peopled only by Hindus, they are living in dreamland. The Hindus, the Mahomedans, the Parsees and the Christians who have made India their country are fellow countrymen, and they will have to live in unity if only for their own interest. In no part of the world are one nationality and one religion synonymous terms: nor has it ever been so in India.

READER: But what about the inborn enmity between Hindus and Mahomedans?

EDITOR: That phrase has been invented by our mutual enemy. When the Hindus and Mahomedans fought against one another, they certainly spoke in that strain. They have long since ceased to fight. How, then, can there be any inborn enmity? Pray remember this, too, that we did not cease to fight only after British occupation. The Hindus flourished under Moslem sovereigns, and Moslems under the Hindu. Each party recognised that mutual fighting was suicidal, and that neither party would abandon its religion by force of arms. Both parties, therefore, decided to live in peace. With the English advent the quarrels recommenced.

The proverbs you have quoted were coined when both were fighting; to quote them now is obviously harmful. Should we not remember that many Hindus and Mahomedans own the same ancestors, and the same blood runs through their veins? Do people become enemies because they change their religion? Is the God of the Mahomedan different from the God of the Hindu? Religions are different roads converging to the same point. What does it matter that we take different roads, so long as we reach the same goal? Wherein is the cause for quarrelling?

Moreover, there are deadly proverbs as between the followers of Shiva and those of Vishnu, yet nobody suggests that these two do not belong to the same nation. It is said that the Vedic religion is different from Jainism, but the followers of the respective faiths are not different nations. The fact is that we have become enslaved, and, therefore, quarrel and like to have our quarrels decided by a third party. There are Hindu iconoclasts as there are Mahomedan. The more we advance in true knowledge, the better we shall understand that we need not be at war with those whose religion we may not follow.

READER: Now I would like to know your views about cow protection.

EDITOR: I myself respect the cow, that is, I look upon her with affectionate reverence. The cow is the protector of India, because, it being an agricultural country, is dependent on the cow's progeny. She is a most useful animal in hundreds of ways. Our Mahomedan brethren will admit this.

But, just as I respect the cow so do I respect my fellow-men. A man is just as useful as a cow, no matter whether he be a Mahomedan or a Hindu. Am I, then to fight with or kill a Mahomedan in order to save a cow? In doing so, I would become an enemy as well of the cow as of the Mahomedan. Therefore, the only method I know of protecting the cow is that I should approach my Mahomedan brother and urge him for the sake of the country to join me in protecting her. If he would not listen to me, I should let the cow go for the simple reason that the matter is beyond my ability. If I were over full of pity for the cow, I should sacrifice my life to save her, but not take my brother's. This, I hold, is the law of our religion.

When men become obstinate, it is a difficult thing. If I pull one way, my Moslem brother will pull another. If I put on a superior air, he will return the compliment. If I bow to him gently, he will do it much, more so, and if he does not, I shall not be considered to have done wrong in having bowed. When the Hindus became insistent, the killing of cows increased. In my opinion, cow protection societies may be considered cow killing societies. It is a disgrace to us that we should need such societies. When we forgot how to protect cows, I suppose we needed such societies.

What am I to do when a blood-brother is on the point of killing a cow? Am I to kill him, or to fall down at his feet and implore him? If you admit that I should adopt the latter course I must do the same to my Moslem brother. Who protects the cow from destruction by Hindus when they cruelly ill-treat her? Whoever reasons with the Hindus when they mercilessly belabour the progeny of the cow with their sticks? But this has not prevented us from remaining one nation.

Lastly, if it be true that the Hindus believe in the doctrine of non-killing, and the Mahomedans do not, what, I pray, is the duty of the former? It is not written that a follower of the religion of Ahimsa (non-killing) may kill a fellow-man. For him the way is straight. In order to save one being, he may not kill another. He can only plead--therein lies his sole duty.

But does every Hindu believe in Ahimsa? Going to the root of the matter, not one man really practises such a religion, because we do destroy life. We are said to follow that religion because we want to obtain freedom from liability to kill any kind of life. Generally speaking, we may observe that many Hindus partake of meat and are not, therefore, followers of Ahimsa.

It is, therefore, preposterous to suggest that the two cannot live together amicably because the Hindus believe in Ahimsa and the Mahomedans do not.

These thoughts are put into our minds by selfish and false religious teachers. The English put the finishing touch. They have a habit of writing history; they pretend to study the manners and customs of all peoples, God has given us a limited mental capacity, but they usurp the function of the Godhead and indulge in novel experiments. They write about their own researches in most laudatory terms and hypnotise us into believing them. We in our ignorance, then fall at their feet.

Those who do not wish to misunderstand things may read up the Koran, and will find therein hundreds of passages acceptable to the Hindus; and the Bhagavad Gita contains passages to which not a Mahomedan can take exception. Am I to dislike a Mahomedan because there are passages in the Koran I do not understand or like? It takes two to make a quarrel. If I do not want to quarrel with a Mahomedan, the latter will be powerless to foist a quarrel on me, and, similarly, I should be powerless if a Mahomedan refuses his assistance to quarrel with me. An arm striking the air will become disjointed. If everyone will try to understand the core of his own religion and adhere to it, and will not allow false teachers to dictate to him, there will be no room left for quarrelling.

READER: But, will the English ever allow the two bodies to join hands?

EDITOR: This question arises out of your timidity. It betrays our shallowness. If two brothers want to live in peace, is it possible for a third party to separate them? If they were to listen to evil counsels, we would consider them to be foolish. Similarly, we Hindus and Mahomedans would have to blame our folly rather than the English, if we allowed them to put asunder. A clay pot would break through impact; if not with one stone, thou with another. The way to save the pot is not to keep it away from the danger point, but to bake it so that no stone would break it. We have then to make our hearts of perfectly baked clay. Then we shall be steeled against all danger. This can be easily done by the Hindus. They are superior in numbers, they pretend that they are more educated, they are, therefore, better able to shield themselves from attack on their amicable relations with the Mahomedans.

There is a mutual distrust between the two communities. The Mahomedans, therefore, ask for certain concessions from Lord Morley. Why should the Hindus oppose this? If the Hindus desisted, the English would notice it, the Mahomedans would gradually begin to trust the Hindus, and brotherliness would be the outcome. We should be ashamed to take our quarrels to the English. Everyone can find out for himself that the Hindus can lose nothing be desisting. The man who has inspired confidence in another has never lost anything in this world.

I do not suggest that the Hindus and the Mahomedans will never fight. Two brothers living together often do so. We shall sometimes have our heads broken. Such a thing ought not to be necessary, but all men are not equi-minded. When people are in a rage, they do many foolish things. These we have to put up with. But, when we do quarrel, we certainly do not want to engage counsel and to resort to English or any law-courts. Two men fight; both have their heads broken, or one only. How shall a third party distribute justice amongst them? Those who fight may expect to be injured.

HINDU-MAHOMEDAN UNITY

Mr. Candler some time ago asked me in an imaginary interview whether if I was sincere in my professions of Hindu-Mahomedan Unity. I would eat and drink with a Mahomedean and give my daughter in marriage to a Mahomedan. This question has been asked again by some friends in another form. Is it necessary for Hindu Mahomedan Unity that there should he interdining and intermarrying? The questioners say that if the two are necessary, real unity can never take place because crores of

Sanatanis

would never reconcile themselves to interdining, much less to intermarriage.

I am one of those who do not consider caste to be a harmful institution. In its origin caste was a wholesome custom and promoted national well-being. In my opinion the idea that interdining or intermarrying is necessary for national growth, is a superstition borrowed from the West. Eating is a process just as vital as the other sanitary necessities of life. And if mankind had not, much to its harm, made of eating a fetish and indulgence we would have performed the operation of eating in private even as one performs the other necessary functions of life in private. Indeed the highest culture in Hinduism regards eating in that light and there are thousands of Hindus still living who will not eat their food in the presence of anybody. I can recall the names of several cultured men and women who ate their food in entire privacy but who never had any illwill against anybody and who lived on the friendliest terms with all.

Intermarriage is a still more difficult question. If brothers and sisters can live on the friendliest footing without ever thinking of marrying each other, I can see no difficulty in my daughter regarding every Mahomedan brother and *vice versa*. I hold strong views on religion and on marriage. The greater the restraint we exercise with regard to our appetites whether about eating or marrying, the better we become from a religious standpoint. I should despair of ever cultivating amicable relations with the world, if I had to recognise the right or the propriety of any young man offering his hand in marriage to my daughter or to regard it as necessary for me to dine with anybody and everybody. I claim that I am living on terms of friendliness with the whole world. I have never quarrelled with a single Mahomedan or Christian but for years I have taken nothing but fruit in Mahomedan or Christian households. I would most certainly decline to eat food cooked from the same plate with my son or to drink water out of a cup which his lips have touched and which has not been washed. But the restraint or the exclusiveness exercised in these matters by me has never affected the closest companionship with the Mahomedan or the Christian friends or my sons.

But interdining and intermarriage have never been a bar to disunion, quarrels and worse. The Pandavas and the Kauravas flew at one another's throats without compunction although they interdined and intermarried. The bitterness between the English and the Germans has not yet died out.

The fact is that intermarriage and interdining are not necessary factors in friendship and unity though they are often emblems thereof. But insistence on either the one or the other can easily become and is to-day a bar to Hindu-Mahomedan Unity. If we make ourselves believe that Hindus and Mahomedans cannot be one unless they interdine or intermarry, we would be creating an artificial barrier between us which it might be almost impossible to remove. And it would seriously interfere with the flowing unity between Hindus and Mahomedans if, for example, Mahomedan youths consider it lawful to court Hindu girls. The Hindu parents will not, even if they suspected any such thing, freely admit Mahomedans to their homes as they have begun to do now. In my opinion it is necessary for Hindu and Mahomedan young men to recognise this limitation.

I hold it to be utterly impossible for Hindus and Mahomedans to intermarry and yet retain intact each other's religion. And the true beauty of Hindu-Mahomedan Unity lies in each remaining true to his own religion and yet being true to each other. For, we are thinking of Hindus and Mahomedans even of the most orthodox type being able to regard one another as natural friends instead of regarding one another as natural enemies as they have done hitherto.

What then does the Hindu-Mahomedan Unity consist in and how can it be best promoted? The answer is simple. It consists in our having a common purpose, a common goal and common sorrows. It is best promoted by co-operating to reach the common goal, by sharing one another's sorrow and by mutual toleration. A common goal we have. We wish this great country of ours to be greater and self-governing.[4] We have enough sorrows to share and to-day seeing that the Mahomedans are deeply touched on the question of Khilafat and their case is just, nothing can be so powerful for winning Mahomedans friendship for the Hindu as to give his whole-hearted support to the Mahomedan claim. No amount of drinking out of the same cup or dining out of the same bowl can bind the two as this help in the Khilafat question.

And mutual toleration is a necessity for all time and for all races. We cannot live in peace if the Hindu will not tolerate the Mahomedan form of worship of God and his manners and customs or if the mahomedans will be impatient of Hindu idolatory, cow-worship. It is not necessary for toleration that I must approve of what I tolerate. I heartily dislike drinking, meat eating and smoking, but I tolerate all these in Hindus, Mahomedans and Christians even as I expect them to tolerate my abstinence from all these, although they may dislike it. All the quarrels between the Hindus and the Mahomedans have arisen from each wanting to *force* the other his view.

HINDU-MUSLIM UNITY

There can be no doubt that successful non-co-operation depends as much on Hindu-Muslim Unity as on non-violence. Greatest strain will be put upon both in the course of the struggle and if it survives that strain, victory is a certainty.

A severe strain was put upon it in Agra and it has been stated that when either party went to the authorities they were referred to Maulana Shaukat

Ali and me. Fortunately there was a far better man at hand. Hakimji Ajmal khan is a devout Muslim who commands the confidence and the respect of both the parties. He with his band of workers hastened to Agra, settled the dispute and the parties became friends as they were never before. An incident occurred nearer Delhi and the same influence worked successfully to avoid what might have become an explosion.

But Hakimji Ajmal khan cannot be everywhere appearing at the exact hour as an angel of peace. Nor can Maulana Shankat Ali or I go everywhere. And yet perfect peace must be observed between the two communities in spite of attempts to divide them.

Why was there any appeal made to the authorities at all at Agra? If we are to work out non-co-operation with any degree of success we must be able to dispense with the protection of the Government when we quarrel among ourselves. The whole scheme of non-co-operation must break to pieces, if our final reliance is to be upon British intervention for the adjustment of our quarrels or the punishment of the guilty ones. In every village and hamlet there must be at least one Hindu and one Muslim, whose primary business must be to prevent quarrels between the two. Some times however, even blood-brothers come to blows. In the initial stages we are bound to do so here and there. Unfortunately we who are public workers have made little attempt to understand and influence the masses and least of all the most turbulent among them. During the process of insinuating ourselves in the estimation of the masses and until we have gained control over the unruly, there are bound to be exhibitions of hasty temper now and then. We must learn at such times to do without an appeal to the Government. Hakimji Ajmal Khan has shown us how to do it.

The union that we want is not a patched up thing but a union of hearts based upon a definite recognition of the indubitable proposition that Swaraj for India must be an impossible dream without an indissoluble union between the Hindus and the Muslims of India. It must not be a mere truce. It cannot be based upon mutual fear. It must be a partnership between equals each respecting the religion of the other.

I would frankly despair of reaching such union if there was anything in the holy Quran enjoining upon the followers of Islam to treat Hindus as their natural enemies or if there was anything in Hinduism to warrant a belief in the eternal enmity between the two.

We would ill learn our history if we conclude that because we have quarrelled in the past, we are destined so to continue unless some such strong power like the British keep us by force of arms from flying at each other's throats. But I am convinced that there is no warrant in Islam or Hinduism for any such belief. True it is that interested fanatical priests in both religions have set the one against the other. It is equally true that Muslim rulers like Christian rulers have used the sword for the propagation of their respective faiths. But in spite of many dark things of the modern times, the world's opinion to-day will as little tolerate forcible conversions as it will tolerate forcible slavery. That probably is the most effective contribution of the scientific spirit of the age. That spirit has revolutionised many a false notion about Christianity as it has about Islam. I do not know a single writer on Islam who defends the use of force in the proselytising process. The influences exerted in our times are far more subtle than that of the sword.

I believe that in the midst of all the bloodshed, chicane and fraud being resorted to on a colossal scale in the west, the whole humanity is silently but surely making progress towards a better age. And India by finding true independence and self-expression through an imperishable Hindu-Muslim unity and through non-violent means, i.e., unadulterated self sacrifice can point a way out of the prevailing darkness.

VI-TREATMENT OF THE DEPRESSED CLASSES

DEPRESSED CLASSES

Vivekanand used to call the Panchamas 'suppressed classes.' There is no doubt that Vivekanand's is a more accurate adjective. We have suppressed them and have consequently become ourselves depressed. That we have become the 'Pariahs of the Empire' is, in Gokhale's language, the retributive justice meted out to us by a just God. A correspondent indignantly asks me in a pathetic letter reproduced elsewhere, what I am doing for them. I have given the letter with the correspondent's own heading. Should not we the Hindus wash our bloodstained hands before we ask the English to wash theirs? This is a proper question reasonably put. And if a member of a slave nation could deliver the suppressed classes from their slavery without freeing myself from my own, I would do so to day. But it is an impossible task. A slave has not the freedom even to do the right thing. It is a right for me to prohibit the importation of foreign goods, but I have no power to bring it about. It was right for Maulana Mahomed Ali to go to Turkey and to tell the Turks personally that India was with them in their righteous struggle. He was not free to do so. If I had a truly national legislative I would answer Hindu insolence by creating special and better wells for the exclusive use of suppressed classes and by erecting better and more numerous schools for them, so that there would be not a single member of the suppressed classes left without a school to teach their children. But I must wait for that better day.

Meanwhile are the depressed classes to be loft to their own resources? Nothing of the sort. In my own humble manner I have done and am doing all I can for my Panchama brother.

There are three courses open to those downtrodden members of the nation. For their impatience they may call in the assistance of the slave owning Government. They will get it but they will fall from the frying pan into the fire. To-day they are slaves of slaves. By seeking Government aid, they will be used for suppressing their kith and kin. Instead of being sinned against, they will themselves be the sinners. The Mussalmans tried it and failed. They found that they were worse off than before. The Sikhs did it unwittingly and failed. To-day there is no more discontented community in India than the Sikhs. Government aid is therefore no solution.

The second is rejection of Hinduism and wholesale conversion to Islam or Christianity. And if a change of religion could be justified for worldly betterment, I would advise it without hesitation. But religion is a matter of the heart. No physical inconvenience can warrant abandonment of one's own religion. If the inhuman treatment of the Panchamas were a part of Hinduism, its rejection would be a paramount duty both for them and for those like me who would not make a fetish even of religion and condone every evil in its sacred name. But, I believe that untouchability is no part of Hinduism. It is rather its excrescence to be removed by every effort. And there is quite an army of Hindu reformers who have set their heart upon ridding Hinduism of this blot. Conversion, therefore, I hold, is no remedy whatsoever.

Then there remains, finally, self-help and self-dependence, with such aid as the non-Panchama Hindus will render of their own motion, not as a matter of patronage but as a matter of duty. And herein comes the use of non-co-operation. My correspondent was correctly informed by Mr. Rajagopaluchari and Mr. Hanumantarao that I would favour well-regulated non-co-operation for this acknowledged evil. But non-co-operation means independence of outside help, it means effort from within. It would not be non-co-operation to insist on visiting prohibited areas. That may be civil disobedience if it is peacefully carried out. But I have found to my cost that civil disobedience requires far greater preliminary training and self-control. All can non-co-operate, but few only can offer civil disobedience. Therefore, by way of protest against Hinduism, the Panchamas can certainly stop all contact and connection with the other Hindus so long as special grievances are maintained. But this means organised intelligent effort. And so far as I can see, there is no leader among the Panchamas who can lead them to victory through non-co-operation.

The better way, therefore, perhaps, is for the Panchamas heartily to join the great national movement that is now going on for throwing off the slavery of the present Government. It is easy enough for the Panchama friends to see that non-co-operation against this evil government presupposes co-operation between the different sections forming the Indian nation. The Hindus must realise that if they wish to offer successful non-co-operation against the Government, they must make common cause with the Panchamas, even as they have made common cause with the Mussalmans. Non-co-operation with it is free from violence, is essentially a movement of intensive self-purification. That process has commenced and whether the

Panchamas deliberately take part in it or not, the rest of the Hindus dare not neglect them without hampering their own progress. Hence though the Panchama problem is as dear to me as life itself, I rest satisfied with the exclusive attention to national non-co-operation. I feel sure that the greater includes the less.

Closely allied to this question is the non-Brahmin question. I wish I had studied it more closely than I have been able to. A quotation from my speech delivered at a private meeting in Madras has been torn from its context and misused to further the antagonism between the so-called Brahmins and the so-called non-Brahmins. I do not wish to retract a word of what I said at that meeting, I was appealing to those who are accepted as Brahmins. I told them that in my opinion the treatment of non-Brahmins by the Brahmins was as satanic as the treatment of us by the British. I added that the non-Brahmins should be placated without any ado or bargaining. But my remarks were never intended to encourage the powerful non-Brahmins of Maharashira or Madras, or the mischievous element among them, to overawe the so-called Brahmins. I use the word 'so-called' advisedly. For the Brahmins who have freed themselves from the thraldom of superstitious orthodoxy have not only no quarrel with non-Brahmins as such, but are in every way eager to advance non-Brahmins wherever they are weak. No lover of his country can possibly achieve its general advance if he dared to neglect the least of his countrymen. Those non-Brahmins therefore who are coqueting with the Government are selling themselves and the nation to which they belong. By all means let those who have faith in the Government help to sustain it, but let no Indian worthy of his birth cut off his nose to spite the face.

AMELIORATION OF THE DEPRESSED CLASSES

The resolution of the Senate of the Gujarat National University in regard to Mr. Andrews' question about the admission of children of the 'depressed' classes to the schools affiliated to that University is reported to have raised a flutter in Ahmedabad. Not only has the flutter given satisfaction to a 'Times of India' correspondent, but the occasion has led to the discovery by him of another defect in the constitution of the Senate in that it does not contain a single Muslim member. The discovery, however, I may inform the reader, is no proof of the want of national character of the University. The Hindu-Muslim unity is no mere lip expression. It requires no artificial proofs. The simple reason why there is no Mussalman representative on the Senate is that no higher educated Mussalman, able to give his time, has been found to take sufficient interest in the national education movement. I merely refer to this matter to show that we must reckon with attempts to discredit the movement even misinterpretation of motives. That is a difficulty from without and easier to deal with.

The 'depressed' classes difficulty is internal and therefore far more serious because it may give rise to a split and weaken the cause--no cause can survive internal difficulties if they are indefinitely multiplied. Yet there can be no surrender in the matter of principles for the avoidance of splits. You cannot promote a cause when you are undermining it by surrendering its vital parts. The depressed classes problem is a vital part of the cause. *Swaraj* is as inconceivable without full reparation to the 'depressed' classes as it is impossible without real Hindu-Muslim unity. In my opinion we have become 'pariahs of the Empire' because we have created 'pariahs' in our midst. The slave owner is always more hurt than the slave. We shall be unfit to gain Swaraj so long as we would keep in bondage a fifth of the population of Hindustan. Have we not made the 'pariah' crawl on his belly? Have we not segregated him? And if it is religion so to treat the 'pariah.' It is the religion of the white race to segregate us. And if it is no argument for the white races to say that we are satisfied with the badge of our inferiority, it is less for us to say that the 'pariah' is satisfied with his. Our slavery is complete when we begin to hug it.

The Gujarat Senate therefore counted the cost when it refused to bend before the storm. This non-co-operation is a process of self-purification. We may not cling to putrid customs and claim the pure boon of *Swaraj*. Untouchability I hold is a custom, not an integral part of Hinduism. The world advanced in thought, though it is still barbarous in action. And no religion can stand that which is not based on fundamental truths. Any glorification of error will destroy a religion as surely as disregard of a disease is bound to destroy a body.

This government of ours is an unscrupulous corporation. It has ruled by dividing Mussalmans from Hindus. It is quite capable of taking advantage of the internal weaknesses of Hinduism. It will set the 'depressed' classes against the rest of the Hindus, non-Brahmins against Brahmins. The Gujarat Senate resolution does not end the trouble. It merely points out the difficulty. The trouble will end only when the masses and classes of Hindus have rid themselves of the sin of untouchability. A Hindu lover of Swaraj will as assiduously work for the amelioration of the lot of the 'depressed' classes as he works for Hindu-Muslim unity. We must treat them as our brothers and give them the same rights that we claim for ourselves.

THE SIN OF UNTOUCHABILITY

It is worthy of note that the subjects Committee accepted without any opposition the clause regarding the sin of untouchability. It is well that the National assembly passed the resolution stating that the removal of this blot on Hinduism was necessary for the attainment of Swaraj. The Devil succeeds only by receiving help from his fellows. He always takes advantage of the weakest spots in our natures in order to gain mastery over us. Even so does the Government retain its control over us through our weaknesses or vices. And if we would render ourselves proof against its machination, we must remove our weaknesses. It is for that reason that I have called non-co-operation a process of purification. As soon as that process is completed, this government must fall to pieces for want of the necessary environment, just as mosquitos cease to haunt a place whose cess-pools are filled up and dried.

Has not a just Nemesis overtaken us for the crime of untouchability? Have we not reaped as we have sown? Have we not practised Dwyerism and O'Dwyerism on our own kith and kin? We have segregated the 'pariah' and we are in turn segregated in the British Colonies. We deny him the use of public wells; we throw the leavings of our plates at him. His very shadow pollutes us. Indeed there is no charge that the 'pariah' cannot fling in our faces and which we do not fling in the faces of Englishmen.

How is this blot on Hinduism to be removed? 'Do unto others as you would that others should do unto you.' I have often told English officials that, if they are friends and servants of India, they should come down from their pedestal, cease to be patrons, demonstrate by their loving deeds that they are in every respect our friends, and believe us to be equals in the same sense they believe fellow Englishmen to be their equals. After the experiences of the Punjab and the Khilafat, I have gone a step further and asked them to repent and to change their hearts. Even so is it necessary for us Hindus to repent of the wrong we have done, to alter our behaviour towards those whom we have 'suppressed' by a system as devilish as we believe the English system of the Government of India to be. We must not throw a few miserable schools at them; we must not adopt the air of superiority towards them. We must treat them as our blood brothers as they are in fact. We must return to them the inheritance of which we have robbed them. And this must not be the act of a few English-knowing reformers merely, but it must be a conscious voluntary effort on the part of the masses. We may not wait till eternity for this much belated reformation. We must aim at bringing it about within this year of grace, probation, preparation and *tapasya*. It is a reform not to follow *Swaraj* but to precede it.

Untouchability is not a sanction of religion, it is a devise of Satan. The devil has always quoted scriptures. But scriptures cannot transcend reason and truth. They are intended to purify reason and illuminate truth. I am not going to burn a spotless horse because the Vedas are reported to have advised, tolerated, or sanctioned the sacrifice. For me the Vedas are divine and unwritten. 'The letter killeth.' It is the spirit that giveth the light. And the spirit of the Vedas is purity, truth, innocence, chastity, humility, simplicity, forgiveness, godliness, and all that makes a man or woman noble and brave. There is neither nobility nor bravery in treating the great and uncomplaining scavengers of the nation as worse than dogs to be despised and spat upon. Would that God gave us the strength and the wisdom to become voluntary scavengers of the nation as the 'suppressed' classes are forced to be. There are Augean stables enough and to spare for us to clean.

VII-TREATMENT OF INDIANS ABROAD

INDIANS ABROAD

The prejudice against Indian settlers outside India is showing itself in a variety of ways: Under the impudent suggestion of sedition the Fiji Government has deported Mr. Manilal Doctor who with his brave and cultured wife has been rendering assistance to the poor indentured Indians of Fiji in a variety of ways. The whole trouble has arisen over the strike of the labourers in Fiji. Indentures have been canceled, but the spirit of slavery is by no means dead. We do not know the genesis of the strike; we do not know that the strikers have done no wrong. But we do know what is behind when a charge of sedition is brought against the strikers and their friends. The readers must remember that the Government that has scented sedition in the recent upheaval in Fiji is the Government that had the hardihood to libel Mr. Andrew's character. What can be the meaning of sedition in connection with the Fiji strikers and Mr. Manilal Doctor? Did they and he want to seize the reins of Government? Did they want any power in that country? They struck for elementary freedom. And it is a prostitution of terms to use the word sedition in such connection. The strikers may have been overhasty. Mr. Manilal Doctor may have misled them. If his advice bordered on the criminal he should have been tried. The information in our possession goes to show that he has been strictly constitutional. Our point, however, is that it is an abuse of power for the Fiji Government to have deported Mr. Manilal Doctor without a trial. It is wrong in principle to deprive a person of his liberty on mere suspicion and without giving him an opportunity of clearing his character. Mr. Manilal Doctor, be it remembered, has for years past made Fiji his home. He has, we believe, bought property there. He has children born in Fiji. Have the children no rights? Has the wife none? May a promising career be ruined at the bidding of a lawless Government? Has Mr. Manilal Doctor been compensated for the losses he must sustain? We trust that the Government of India which has endeavoured to protect the rights of Indian settlers abroad will take up the question of Mr. Doctor's deportation.

Nor is Fiji the only place where the spirit of lawlessness among the powerful has come to the surface. Indians of (the late) German East Africa find themselves in a worse position than heretofore. They state that even their property is not safe. They have to pay all kinds of dues on passports. They are hampered in their trade. They are not able even to send money orders.

In British East Africa the cloud is perhaps the thickest. The European settlers there are doing their utmost to deprive the Indian settlers of practically every right they have hitherto possessed. An attempt is being made to compass their ruin both by legislative enactment and administrative action.

In South Africa every Indian who has anything to do with that part of the British Dominions is watching with bated breath the progress of commission that is now sitting.

The Government of India have no easy job in protecting the interests of Indian settlers in these various parts of His Majesty's dominions. They will be able to do so only by following the firmest and the most consistent policy. Justice is admittedly on the side of the Indian settlers. But they are the weak party. A strong agitation in India followed by strong action by the Government of India can alone save the situation.

INDIANS OVERSEAS

The meeting held at the Excelsior Theatre in Bombay to pass resolutions regarding East Africa and Fiji, and presided over by Sir Narayan Chandavarkar, was an impressive gathering. The Theatre was filled to overflowing. Mr. Andrews' speech made clear what is needed. Both the political and the civil rights of Indians of East Africa are at stake. Mr. Anantani, himself an East African settler, showed in a forceful speech that the Indians were the pioneer settlers. An Indian sailor named Kano directed the celebrated Vasco De Gama to India. He added amid applause that Stanley's expedition for the search and relief of Dr. Livingstone was also fitted out by Indians. Indian workmen had built the Uganda Railway at much peril to their lives. An Indian contractor had taken the contract.

Indian artisans had supplied the skill. And now their countrymen were in danger of being debarred from its use.

The uplands of East Africa have been declared a Colony and the lowlands a Protectorate. There is a sinister significance attached to the declaration. The Colonial system gives the Europeans larger powers. It will tax all the resources of the Government of India to prevent the healthy uplands from becoming a whiteman's preserve and the Indians from being relegated to the swampy lowlands.

The question of franchise will soon become a burning one. It will be suicidal to divide the electorate or to appoint Indians by nomination. There must be one general electoral roll applying the same qualifications to all the voters. This principle, as Mr. Andrews reminded the meeting, had worked well at the Cape.

The second part of the East African resolution shows the condition of our countrymen in the late German East Africa. Indian soldiers fought there and now the position of Indians is worse than under German rule. H.H. the Agakhan suggested that German East Africa should be administered from India. Sir Theodore Morison would have couped up all Indians in German East Africa. The result was that both the proposals went by the board and the expected has happened. The greed of the English speculator has prevailed and he is trying to squeeze out the Indian. What will the Government of India protect? Has it the will to do so? Is not India itself being exploited? Mr. Jehangir Petit recalled the late Mr. Gokhale's views that we were not to expect a full satisfaction regarding the status of our countrymen across the seas until we had put our own house in order. Helots in our own country, how could we do better outside? Mr. Petit wants systematic and severe retaliation. In my opinion, retaliation is a double-edged weapon. It does not fail to hurt the user if it also hurts the party against whom it is used. And who is to give effect to retaliation? It is too much to expect an English Government to adopt effective retaliation against their own people. They will expostulate, they will remonstrate, but they will not go to war with their own Colonies. For the logical outcome of retaliation must mean war, if retaliation will not answer.

Let us face the facts frankly. The problem is difficult alike for Englishmen and for us. The Englishmen and Indians do not agree in the Colonies. The Englishmen do not want us where they can live. Their civilisation is different from ours. The two cannot coalesce until there is mutual respect.

The Englishman considers himself to belong to the ruling race. The Indian struggles to think that he does not belong to the subject race and in the very act of thinking admits his subjection. We must then attain equality at home before we can make any real impression abroad.

This is not to say that we must not strive to do better abroad whilst we are ill at ease in our own home. We must preserve, we must help our countrymen who have settled outside India. Only if we recognise the true situation, we and our countrymen abroad will learn to be patient and know that our chief energy must be concentrated on a betterment of our position at home. If we can raise our status here to that of equal partners not in name but in reality so that every Indian might feel it, all else must follow as a matter of course.

PARIAHS OF THE EMPIRE

The memorable Conference at Gujrat in its resolution on the status of Indians abroad has given it as its opinion that even this question may become one more reason for non-co-operation. And so it may. Nowhere has there been such open defiance of every canon of justice and propriety as in the shameless decision of confiscation of Indian rights in the Kenia Colony announced by its Governor. This decision has been supported by Lord Milnor and Mr. Montagu. And his Indian colleagues are satisfied with the decision. Indians, who have made East Africa, who out-number the English, are deprived practically of the right of representation on the Council. They are to be segregated in parts not habitable by the English. They are to have neither the political nor the material comfort. They are to become 'Pariahs' in a country made by their own labour, wealth and intelligence. The Viceroy is pleased to say that he does not like the outlook and is considering the steps to be taken to vindicate the justice. He is not met with a new situation. The Indians of East Africa had warned him of the impending doom. And if His Excellency has not yet found the means of ensuring redress, he is not likely to do it in future. I would respectfully ask his Indian colleagues whether they can stand this robbery of their countrymen rights.

In South Africa the situation is not less disquieting. My misgivings seem to be proving true, and repatriation is more likely to prove compulsory than voluntary. It is a response to the anti-Asiatic agitation, not a measure of relief for indigent Indians. It looks very like a trap laid for the unwary Indian. The Union Government appears to be taking an unlawful advantage of a section of a relieving law designed for a purpose totally different from the one now intended.

As for Fiji, the crime against humanity is evidently to be hushed up. I do hope that unless an inquiry is to be made into the Fiji Martial Law doings, no Indian member will undertake to go to Fiji. The Government of India appear to have given an undertaking to send Indian labour to Fiji provided the commission that was to proceed there in order to investigate the condition on the spot returns with a favourable report.

For British Guiana I observe from the papers received from that quarter, that the mission that came here is already declaring that Indian labour will be forthcoming from India. There seems to me to be no real prospect for Indian enterprise in that part of the world. We are not wanted in any part of the British Dominion except as Pariahs to do the scavenging for the European settlers.

The situation is clear. We are Pariahs in our own home. We get only what Government intend to give, not what we demand and have a right to. We may get the crumbs, never the loaf. I have seen large and tempting crumbs from a lavish table. And I have seen the eyes of our Pariahs--the shame of Hinduism--brightening to see those heavy crumbs filling their baskets. But the superior Hindu, who is filling the basket from a safe distance, knows that they are unfit for his own consumption. And so we in our turn may receive even Governorships which the real rulers no longer require or which they cannot retain with safety for their material interest--the political and material hold on India. It is time we realised our true status.

VIII-NON-CO-OPERATION

A writer in the "Times of India," the Editor of that wonderful daily and Mrs. Besant have all in their own manner condemned non-co-operation conceived in connection with the Khilafat movement. All the three writings naturally discuss many side issues which I shall omit for the time being. I propose to answer two serious objections raised by the writers. The sobriety with which they are stated entitles them to a greater consideration than if they had been given in violent language. In non-co-operation, the writers think, it would be difficult if not impossible to avoid violence. Indeed violence, the "Times of India" editorial says, has already commenced in that ostracism has been resorted to in Calcutta and Delhi. Now I fear that ostracism to a certain extent is impossible to avoid. I remember in South Africa in the initial stages of the passive resistance campaign those who had fallen away were ostracised. Ostracism is violent or peaceful in according to the manner in which it is practised. A congregation may well refuse to recite prayers after a priest who prizes his title above his honour. But the ostracism will become violent if the individual life of a person is made unbearable by insults innuendoes or abuse. The real danger of violence lies in the people resorting to non-co-operation becoming impatient and revengeful. This may happen, if, for instance, payment of taxes is suddenly withdrawn or if pressure is put upon soldiers to lay down their arms. I however do not fear any evil consequences, for the simple reason that every responsible Mahomedan understands that non-co-operation to be successful must be totally unattended with violence. The other objection raised is that those who may give up their service may have to starve. That is just a possibility but a remote one, for the committee will certainly make due provision for those who may suddenly find themselves out of employment. I propose however to examine the whole of the difficult question much more fully in a future issue and hope to show that if Indian-Mahomedan feeling is to be respected, there is nothing left but non-co-operation if the decision arrived at is adverse.

MR. MONTAGU ON THE KHILAFAT AGITATION

Mr. Montagu does not like the Khilafat agitation that is daily gathering force. In answer to questions put in the House of Commons, he is reported to have said that whilst he acknowledged that I had rendered distinguished services to the country in the past, he could not look upon my present attitude with equanimity and that it was not to be expected that I could now be treated as leniently as I was during the Rowlatt Act agitation. He added that he had every confidence in the central and the local Governments, that they were carefully watching the movement and that they had full power to deal with the situation.

This statement of Mr. Montagu has been regarded in some quarters as a threat. It has even been considered to be a blank cheque for the Government of India to re-establish the reign of terror if they chose. It is certainly inconsistent with his desire to base the Government on the goodwill of the people. At the same time if the Hunter Committee's finding be true and if I was the cause of the disturbances last year, I was undoubtedly treated with exceptional leniency, I admit too that my activity this year is fraught with greater peril to the Empire as it is being conducted to-day than was last year's activity. Non-co-operation in itself is more harmless than civil disobedience, but in its effect it is far more dangerous for the Government than civil disobedience. Non-co-operation is intended so far to paralyse the Government, as to compel justice from it. If it is carried to the extreme point, it can bring the Government to a standstill.

A friend who has been listening to my speeches once asked me whether I did not come under the sedition section of the Indian Penal Code. Though I had not fully considered it, I told him that very probably I did and that I could not plead 'not guilty' if I was charged under it. For I must admit that I can pretend to no 'affection' for the present Government. And my speeches are intended to create 'disaffection' such that the people might consider it a shame to assist or co-operate with a Government that had forfeited all title to confidence, respect or support.

I draw no distinction between the Imperial and the Indian Government. The latter has accepted, on the Khilafat, the policy imposed upon it by the former. And in the Punjab case the former has endorsed the policy of terrorism and emasculation of a brave people initiated by the latter. British ministers have broken their pledged word and wantonly wounded the feelings of the seventy million Mussulmans of India. Innocent men and women were insulted by the insolent officers of the Punjab Government. Their wrongs not only unrighted but the very officers who so cruelly subjected them to barbarous humiliation retain office under the Government.

When at Amritsar last year I pleaded with all the earnestness I could command for co-operation with the Government and for response to the wishes expressed in the Royal Proclamation; I did so because I honestly believed that a new era was about to begin, and that the old spirit of fear, distrust and consequent terrorism was about to give place to the new spirit of respect, trust and good-will. I sincerely believed that the Mussalman sentiment would be placated and that the officers that had misbehaved during the Martial Law regime in the Punjab would be at least dismissed and the people would be otherwise made to feel that a Government that had always been found quick (and rightly) to punish popular excesses would not fail to punish its agents' misdeeds. But to my amazement and dismay I have discovered that the present representatives of the Empire have become dishonest and unscrupulous. They have no real regard for the wishes of the people of India and they count Indian honour as of little consequence.

I can no longer retain affection for a Government so evilly manned as it is now-a-days. And for me, it is humiliating to retain my freedom and be a witness to the continuing wrong. Mr. Montagu however is certainly right in threatening me with deprivation of my liberty if I persist in endangering the existence of the Government. For that must be the result if my activity bears fruit. My only regret is that inasmuch as Mr. Montagu admits my past services, he might have perceived that there must be something exceptionally bad in the Government if a well-wisher like me could no longer give his affection to it. It was simpler to insist on justice being done to the Mussulmans and to the Punjab than to threaten me with punishment so that the injustice might be perpetuated. Indeed I fully expect it will be found that even in promoting disaffection towards an unjust Government I have rendered greater services to the Empire than I am already credited with.

At the present moment, however, the duty of those who approve of my activity is clear. They ought on no account to resent the deprivation of my liberty, should the Government of India deem it to be their duty to take it away. A citizen has no right to resist such restriction imposed in accordance with the laws of the State to which he belongs. Much less have those who sympathize with him. In my case there can be no question of sympathy. For I deliberately oppose the Government to the extent of trying to put its very existence in jeopardy. For my supporters, therefore, it must be a moment of joy when I am imprisoned. It means the beginning of success if only the supporters continue the policy for which I stand. If the Government arrest me, they would do so in order to stop the progress of non-co-operation which I preach. It follows that if non-co-operation continues with unabated vigour, even after my arrest, the Government must imprison others or grant the people's wish in order to gain their co-operation. Any eruption of violence on the part of the people even under provocation would end in disaster. Whether therefore it is I or any one else who is arrested during the campaign, the first condition of success is that there must be no resentment shown against it. We cannot imperil the very existence of a Government and quarrel with its attempt to save itself by punishing those who place it in danger.

AT THE CALL OF THE COUNTRY

Dr. Sapru delivered before the Khilafat Conference at Allahabad an impassioned address sympathising with the Mussulmans in their trouble but dissuaded them from embarking on non-co-operation. He was frankly unable to suggest a substitute but was emphatically of opinion that whether there was a substitute or not non-co-operation was a remedy worse than the disease. He said further that Mussulmans will be taking upon their shoulders, a serious responsibility, if whilst they appealed to the ignorant masses to join them, they could not appeal to the Indian judges to resign and if they did they would not succeed.

I acknowledge the force of Dr. Sapru's last argument. At the back of Dr. Sapru's mind is the fear that non-co-operation by the ignorant people would lead to distress and chaos and would do no good. In my opinion any non-co-operation is bound to do some good. Even the Viceragal door-keeper saying, 'Please Sir, I can serve the Government no longer because it has hurt my national honour' and resigning is a step mightier and more effective than the mightiest speech declaiming against the Government for its injustice.

Nevertheless it would be wrong to appeal to the door-keeper until one has appealed to the highest in the land. And as I propose, if the necessity arose, to ask the door-keepers of the Government to dissociate themselves from an unjust Government I propose now to address, an appeal to the Judges and the Executive Councillors to join the protest that is rising from all over India against the double wrong done to India, on the Khilafat and the Punjab question. In both, national honour is involved.

I take it that these gentlemen have entered upon their high offices not for the sake of emolument, nor I hope for the sake of fame, but for the sake of serving their country. It was not for money, for they were earning more than they do now. It must not be for fame, for they cannot buy fame at the cost of national honour. The only consideration, that can at the present moment keep them in office must be service of the country.

When the people have faith in the government, when it represents the popular will, the judges and the executive officials possibly serve the country. But when that government does not represent the will of the people, when it supports dishonesty and terrorism, the judges and the executive officials by retaining office become instrument of dishonesty and terrorism. And the least therefore that these holders of high offices can do is to cease to become agents of a dishonest and terrorising government.

For the judges, the objection will be raised that they are above politics, and so they are and should be. But the doctrine is true only in so far as the government is on the whole for the benefit of the people and at least represents the will of the majority. Not to take part in politics means not to take sides. But when a whole country has one mind, one will, when a whole country has been denied justice, it is no longer a question of party politics, it is a matter of life and death. It then becomes the duty of every citizen to refuse to serve a government which misbehaves and flouts national wish. The judges are at that moment bound to follow the nation if they are ultimately its servants.

There remains another argument to be examined. It applies to both the judges and the members of the executive. It will be urged that my appeal could only be meant for the Indians and what good can it do by Indians renouncing offices which have been won for the nation by hard struggle. I wish that I could make an effective appeal to the English as well as the Indians. But I confess that I have written with the mental reservation that the appeal is addressed only to the Indians. I must therefore examine the argument just stated. Whilst it is true that these offices have been secured after a prolonged struggle, they are of use not because of the struggle, but because they are intended to serve the nation. The moment they cease to possess that quality, they become useless and as in the present case harmful, no matter how hard-earned and therefore valuable they may have been at the outset.

I would submit too to our distinguished countrymen who occupy high offices that their giving up will bring the struggle to a speedy end and would probably obviate the danger attendant upon the masses being called upon to signify their disapproval by withdrawing co-operation. If the titleholders gave up their titles, if the holders of honorary offices gave up their appointment and if the high officials gave up their posts, and the would-be councillors boycotted the councils, the Government would quickly come to its senses and give effect to the people's will. For the alternative before the Government then would be nothing but despotic rule pure and simple. That would probably mean military dictatorship. The world's opinion has advanced so far that Britain dare not contemplate such dictatorship with equanimity. The taking of the steps suggested by me will constitute the peacefullest revolution the world has ever seen. Once the infallibility of non-co-operation is realised, there is an end to all bloodshed and violence in any shape or form.

Undoubtedly a cause must be grave to warrant the drastic method of national non-co-operation. I do say that the affront such as has been put upon Islam cannot be repeated for a century. Islam must rise now or 'be fallen' if not for ever, certainly for a century. And I cannot imagine a graver wrong than the massacre of Jallianwalla and the barbarity that followed it, the whitewash by the Hunter Committee, the dispatch of the Government of India, Mr. Montagu's letter upholding the Viceroy and the then Lieutenant Governor of the Punjab, the refusal to remove officials who made of the lives of the Punjabis 'a hell' during the Martial Law period. These act constitute a complete series of continuing wrongs against India which if India has any sense of honour, she must right at the sacrifice of all the material wealth she possesses. If she does not, she will have bartered her soul for a 'mess of pottage.'

NON-CO-OPERATION EXPLAINED

> A representative of Madras Mail called on Mr. M.K. Gandhi at his temporary residence in the Pursewalkam High road for an interview on the subject of non-co-operation. Mr. Gandhi, who has come to Madras on a tour to some of the principal Muslim centres in Southern India, was busy with a number of workers discussing his programme; but he expressed his readiness to answer questions on the chief topic which is agitating Muslims and Hindus.

"After your experience of the Satyagraha agitation last year, Mr. Gandhi, are you still hopeful and convinced of the wisdom of advising non-co-operation?"--"Certainly."

"How do you consider conditions have altered since the Satyagraha movement of last year?"--"I consider that people are better disciplined now than they were before. In this I include even the masses who I have had opportunities of seeing in large numbers in various parts of the country."

"And you are satisfied that the masses understand the spirit of Satyagraha?"--"Yes."

"And that is why you are pressing on with the programme of non-co-operation?"--"Yes. Moreover, the danger that attended the civil disobedience part of Satyagraha does not apply to non-co-operation, because in non-co-operation we are not taking up civil disobedience of laws as a mass movement. The result hitherto has been most encouraging. For instance, people in Sindh and Delhi in spite of the irritating restrictions upon their liberty by the authorities have carried out the Committee's instructions in regard to the Seditious Meetings Proclamation and to the prohibition of posting placards on the walls which we hold to be inoffensive but which the authorities consider to be offensive."

"What is the pressure which you expect to bring to bear on the authorities if co-operation is withdrawn?"--"I believe, and everybody must grant, that no Government can exist for a single moment without the co-operation of the people, willing or forced, and if people suddenly withdraw their co-operation in every detail, the Government will come to a stand-still."

"But is there not a big 'If' in it?"--"Certainly there is."

"And how do you propose to succeed against the big 'If'?"--"In my plan of campaign expediency has no room. If the Khilafat movement has really permeated the masses and the classes, there must be adequate response from the people."

"But are you not begging the question?"--"I am not begging the question, because so far as the data before me go, I believe that the Muslims keenly feel the Khilafat grievance. It remains to be seen whether their feeling is intense enough to evoke in them the measure of sacrifice adequate for successful non-co-operation."

"That is, your survey of the conditions, you think, justifies your advising non-co-operation in the full conviction that you have behind you the support of the vast masses of the Mussalman population?"--"Yes."

"This non-co-operation, you are satisfied, will extend to complete severance of co-operation with the Government?"--No; nor is it at the present moment my desire that it should. I am simply practising non-co-operation to the extent that is necessary to make the Government realise the depth of popular feeling in the matter and the dissatisfaction with the Government that all that could be done has not been done either by the Government of India or by the Imperial Government, whether on the Khilafat question or on the "Punjab question."

"Do you Mr. Gandhi, realise that even amongst Mahomedans there are sections of people who are not enthusiastic over non-co-operation however much they may feel the wrong that has been done to their community?"--"Yes. But their number is smaller than those who are prepared to adopt non-co-operation."

"And yet does not the fact that there has not been an adequate response to your appeal for resignation of titles and offices and for boycott of elections of the Councils indicate that you may be placing more faith in their strength of conviction than is warranted?"--"I think not; for the reason that the stage has only just come into operation and our people are always most cautious and slow to move. Moreover, the first stage largely affects the uppermost strata of society, who represent a microscopic minority though they are undoubtedly an influential body of people."

"This upper class, you think, has sufficiently responded to your appeal?"--"I am unable to say either one way or the other at present. I shall be able to give a definite answer at the end of this month."...

"Do you think that without one's loyalty to the King and the Royal Family being questioned, one can advocate non-co-operation in connection with the Royal visit?" "Most decidedly; for the simple reason that if there is any disloyalty about the proposed boycott of the Prince's visit, it is disloyalty to the Government of the day and not to the person of His Royal highness."

"What do you think is to be gained by promoting this boycott in connection with the Royal visit?"--"Because I want to show that the people of India are not in sympathy with the Government of the day and that they strongly disapprove of the policy of the Government in regard to the Punjab and Khilafat, and even in respect of other important administrative measures. I consider that the visit of the Prince of Wales is a singularly good opportunity to the people to show their disapproval of the present Government. After all, the visit is calculated to have tremendous political results. It is not to be a non-political event, and seeing that the Government of India and the Imperial Government want to make the visit a political event of first class importance, namely, for the purpose of strengthening their hold upon India, I for one, consider that it is the bounden duty of the people to boycott the visit which is being engineered by the two Governments in their own interest which at the present moment is totally antagonistic to the people."

"Do you mean that you want this boycott promoted because you feel that the strengthening of the hold upon India is not desirable in the best interests of the country?"--"Yes. The strengthening of the hold of a Government so wicked as the present one is not desirable for the best interests of the people. Not that I want the bond between England and India to become loosened for the sake of loosening it but I want that bond to become strengthened only in so far as it adds to the welfare of India."

"Do you think that non-co-operation and the non-boycott of the Legislative Councils consistent?"--"No; because a person who takes up the programme of non-co-operation cannot consistently stand for Councils."

"Is non-co-operation, in your opinion, an end in itself or a means to an end, and if so, what is the end?" "It is a means to an end, the end being to make the present Government just, whereas it has become mostly unjust. Co-operation with a just Government is a duty; non-co-operation with an unjust Government is equally a duty."

"Will you look with favour upon the proposal to enter the Councils and to carry on either obstructive tactics or to decline to take the oath of allegiance consistent with your non-co-operation?"--"No; as an accurate student of non-co-operation, I consider that such a proposal is inconsistent with the true spirit of non-co-operation. I have often said that a Government really thrives on obstruction and so far as the proposal not to take the oath of allegiance is concerned, I can really see no meaning in it; it amounts to a useless waste of valuable time and money."

"In other words, obstruction is no stage in non-co-operation?" --"No,"....

"Are you satisfied that all efforts at constitutional agitation have been exhausted and that non-co-operation is the only course left us?" "I do not consider non-co-operation to be unconstitutional remedies now left open to us, non-co-operation is the only one left for us." "Do you consider it constitutional to adopt it with a view merely to paralyse Government?"--"Certainly, it is not unconstitutional, but a prudent man will not take all the steps that are constitutional if they are otherwise undesirable, nor do I advise that course. I am resorting to non-co-operation in progressive stages because I want to evolve true order out of untrue order. I am not going to take a single step in non-co-operation unless I am satisfied that the country is ready for that step, namely, non-co-operation will not be followed by anarchy or disorder."

"How will you satisfy yourself anarchy will not follow?"

"For instance, if I advise the police to lay down their arms, I shall have satisfied myself that we are able by voluntary assistance to protect ourselves against thieves and robbers. That was precisely what was done in Lahore and Amritsar last year by the citizens by means of volunteers when the Military and the police had withdrawn. Even where Government had not taken such measures in a place, for want of adequate force, I know people have successfully protected themselves."

"You have advised lawyers to non-co-operate by suspending their practice. What is your experience? Has the lawyers' response to your appeal encouraged you to hope that you will be able to carry through all stages of non-co-operation with the help of such people?"

"I cannot say that a large number has yet responded to my appeal. It is too early to say how many will respond. But I may say that I do not rely merely upon the lawyer class or highly educated men to enable the Committee to carry out all the stages of non-co-operation. My hope lies more with the masses so far as the later stages of non-co-operation are concerned."

August 1920.

RELIGIOUS AUTHORITY FOR NON-CO-OPERATION

It is not without the greatest reluctance that I engage in a controversy with so learned a leader like Sir Narayan Chandavarkar. But in view of the fact that I am the author of the movement of non-co-operation, it becomes my painful duty to state my views even though they are opposed to those of the leaders whom I look upon with respect. I have just read during my travels in Malabar Sir Narayan's rejoinder to my answer to the Bombay manifesto against non-co-operation. I regret to have to say that the rejoinder leaves me unconvinced. He and I seem to read the teachings of the Bible, the Gita and the Koran from different standpoints or we put different interpretations on them. We seem to understand the words Ahimsa, politics and religion differently. I shall try my best to make clear my meaning of the common terms and my reading of the different religious.

At the outset let me assure Sir Narayan that I have not changed my views on Ahimsa. I still believe that man not having been given the power of creation does not possess the right of destroying the meanest creature that lives. The prerogative of destruction belongs solely to the creator of all that lives. I accept the interpretation of Ahimsa, namely, that it is not merely a negative State of harmlessness, but it is a positive state of love, of doing good even to the evil-doer. But it does not mean helping the evil-doer to continue the wrong or tolerating it by passive acquiescence. On the contrary love, the active state of Ahimsa, requires you to resist the wrong-doer by dissociating yourself from him even though it may offend him or injure him physically. Thus if my son lives a life of shame, I may not help him to do so by continuing to support him; on the contrary, my love for him requires me to withdraw all support from him although it may mean even his death. And the same love imposes on me the obligation of welcoming him to my bosom when he repents. But I may not by physical force compel my son to become good. That in my opinion is the moral of the story of the Prodigal Son.

Non-co-operation is not a passive state, it is an intensely active state--more active than physical resistance or violence. Passive resistance is a misnomer. Non-co-operation in the sense used by me must be non-violent and therefore neither punitive nor vindictive nor based on malice ill-will or hatred. It follows therefore that it would be sin for me to serve General Dyer and co-operate with him to shoot innocent men. But it will be an exercise of forgiveness or love for me to nurse him back to life, if he was suffering from a physical malady. I cannot use in this context the word co-operation as Sir Narayan would perhaps use it. I would co-operate a thousand times with this Government to wean it from its career of crime but I will not for a single moment co-operate with it to continue that career. And I would be guilty of wrong doing if I retained a title from it or "a service under it or supported its law-courts or schools." Better for me a beggar's bowl than the richest possession from hands stained with the blood of the innocents of Jallianwala. Better by far a warrant of imprisonment than honeyed words from those who have wantonly wounded the religious sentiment of my seventy million brothers.

My reading of the Gita is diametrically opposed to Sir Narayan's. I do not believe that the Gita teaches violence for doing good. It is pre-eminently a description of the duel that goes on in our own hearts. The divine author has used a historical incident for inculcating the lesson of doing one's duty even at the peril of one's life. It inculcates performance of duty irrespective of the consequences, for, we mortals, limited by our physical frames, are incapable of controlling actions save our own. The Gita distinguishes between the powers of light and darkness and demonstrates their incompatibility.

Jesus, in my humble opinion, was a prince among politicians. He did render unto Caesar that which was Caesar's. He gave the devil his due. He ever shunned him and is reported never once to have yielded to his incantations. The politics of his time consisted in securing the welfare of the people by teaching them not to be seduced by the trinkets of the priests and the pharisees. The latter then controlled and moulded the life of the people. To-day the system of government is so devised as to affect every department of our life. It threatens our very existence. If therefore we want to conserve the welfare of the nation, we must religiously interest ourselves in the doing of the governors and exert a moral influence on them by insisting on their obeying the laws of morality. General Dyer did produce a 'moral effect' by an act of butchery. Those who are engaged in forwarding the movement of non-co-operation, hope to produce a moral effect by a process of self-denial, self-sacrifice and self-purification. It surprises me that Sir Narayan should speak of General Dyer's massacre in the same breath as acts of non-co-operation. I have done my best to understand his meaning, but I am sorry to confess that I have failed.

THE INWARDNESS OF NON-CO-OPERATION

I commend to the attention of the readers the thoughtful letter received from Miss Anne Marie Peterson. Miss Peterson is a lady who has been in India for some years and has closely followed Indian affairs. She is about to sever her connection with her mission for the purpose of giving herself to education that is truly national.

I have not given the letter in full. I have omitted all personal references. But her argument has been left entirely untouched. The letter was not meant to be printed. It was written just after my Vellore speech. But it being intrinsically important, I asked the writer for her permission, which she gladly gave, for printing it.

I publish it all the more gladly in that it enables me to show that the movement of non-co-operation is neither anti-Christian nor anti-English nor anti-European. It is a struggle between religion and irreligion, powers of light and powers of darkness.

It is my firm opinion that Europe to-day represents not the spirit of God or Christianity but the spirit of Satan. And Satan's successes are the greatest when he appears with the name of God on his lips. Europe is to-day only nominally Christian. In reality it is worshipping Mammon. 'It is easier for a camel to pass through the eye of a needle than for a rich man to enter the kingdom.' Thus really spoke Jesus Christ. His so-called followers measure their moral progress by their material possessions. The very national anthem of England is anti-Christian. Jesus who asked his followers to love their enemies even as themselves, could not have sung of his enemies, 'confound his enemies frustrate their knavish tricks.' The last book that Dr. Wallace wrote set forth his deliberate conviction that the much vaunted advance of science had added not an inch to the moral stature of Europe. The last war however has shown, as nothing else has, the Satanic nature of the civilization that dominates Europe to day. Every canon of public morality has been broken by the victors in the name of virtue. No lie has been considered too foul to be uttered. The motive behind every crime is not religious or spiritual but grossly material. But the Mussalmans and the Hindus who are struggling against the Government have religion and honour as their motive. Even the cruel assassination which has just shocked the country is reported to have a religious motive behind it. It is certainly necessary to purge religion of its excrescences, but it is equally necessary to expose the hollowness of moral pretensions on the part of those who prefer material wealth to moral gain. It is easier to wean an ignorant fanatic from his error than a confirmed scoundrel from his scoundrelism.

This however is no indictment against individuals or even nations. Thousands of individual Europeans are rising above their environment. I write of the tendency in Europe as reflected in her present leaders. England through her leaders is insolently crushing Indian religious and national sentiment under her heels. England under the false plea of self-determination is trying to exploit the oil fields of Mesopotamia which she is almost to leave because she has probably no choice. France through her leaders is lending her name to training Cannibals as soldiers and is shamelessly betraying her trust as a mandatory power by trying to kill the spirit of the Syrians. President Wilson has thrown on the scrap heap his precious fourteen points.

It is this combination of evil forces which India is really fight through non-violent non-cooperation. And those like Miss Peters whether Christian or European, who feel that this error must be dethron can exercise the privilege of doing so by joining the non-co-operatic movement. With the honour of Islam is bound up the safety of religion itse and with the honour of India is bound up the honour of every nation know to be weak.

A MISSIONARY ON NON-CO-OPERATION

The following letter has been received by Mr. Gandhi from Miss Anne Marie Peterson of the Danish Mission in Madras:--

Dear Mr. Gandhi,

I cannot thank you enough for your kindness and the way in which you received me and I feel that meeting more or less decided my future. I have thrown myself at the feet of India. At the same time I know that in Christ alone is my abode and I have no longing and no desire but to live Him, my crucified Saviour, and reveal Him for those with whom I come in contact. I just cling to his feet and pray with tears that I may not disgrace him as we Christians have been doing by our behaviour in India. We go on crucifying Christ while we long to proclaim the Power of His resurrection by which He has conquered untruth and unrighteousness. If we who bear His name were true to Him, we would never bow ourselves before the Powers of this world, but we would always be on the side of the poor, the suffering and the oppressed. But we are not and therefore I feel myself under obligation and only to Christ but to India for His sake at this time of momentous importance for her future.

Truly it matters little what I, a lonely and insignificant person, may say or do. What is my protest against the common current, the race to which I belong is taking and (what grieves me more), which the missionary societies seem to follow? Even if a respectable number protested it would not be of any use. Yet were I alone against the whole world, I must follow my conscience and my God.

I therefore cannot but smile when I see people saying, you should have awaited the decision of the National Congress before starting the non-co-operation movement. You have a message for the country, and the Congress is the voice of the nation--its servant and not its master. A majority has no right simply because it is a majority.

But we must try to win the majority. And it is easy to see that now that Congress is going to be with you. Would it have done so if you had kept quiet and not lent your voice to the feelings of the people? Would the Congress have known its mind? I think not.

I myself was in much doubt before I heard you. But you convinced me. Not that I can feel much on the question of the Khilafat. I cannot. I can see what service you are doing to India, if you can prevent the Mahomedans from using the sword in order to take revenge and get their rights. I can see that if you unite the Hindus and the Mahomedans, it will be a master stroke. How I wish the Christian would also come forward and unite with you for the sake of their country and the honour not only of their Motherland but of Christ. I may not feel much for Turkey, but I feel for India, and I can see she (India) has no other way to protest against being trampled down and crushed than non-co-operation.

I also want you to know that many in Denmark and all over the world, yes, I am sure every true Christian, will feel with and be in sympathy with India in the struggle which is now going on. God forbid that in the struggle between might and right, truth and untruth, the spirit and the flesh, there should be a division of races. There is not. The same struggle is going on all over the world. What does it matter then that we are a few? God is on our side.

Brute force often seems to get the upper hand but righteousness always has and always shall conquer, be it even through much suffering, and what may even appear to be a defeat. Christ conquered, when the world crucified Him. Blessed are the meek; they shall inherit the earth.

When I read your speech given at Madras it struck me that it should be printed as a pamphlet in English, Tamil, Hindustani and all the most used languages and then spread to every nook and corner of India.

The non-co-operation movement once started must be worked so as to become successful. If it is not, I dread to think of the consequences. But you cannot expect it to win in a day or two. It must take time and you will not despair if you do not reach your goal in a hurry. For those who have faith there is no haste.

Now for the withdrawal of the children and students from Government schools, I think, it a most important step. Taking the Government help (even if it be your money they pay you back), we must submit to its scheme, its rules and regulation. India and we who love her have come to the conclusion that the education the foreign Government has given you is not healthy for India and can certainly never make for her real growth. This movement would lead to a spontaneous rise of national schools. Let them be a few but let them spring up through self-sacrifice. Only by indigenous education can India be truly uplifted. Why this appeals so much to me is perhaps

because I belong to the part of the Danish people who started their own independent, indigenous national schools. The Danish Free Schools and Folk-High-Schools, of which you may have heard, were started against the opposition and persecution of the State. The organisers won and thus have regenerated the nation. With my truly heartfelt thanks and prayers for you.

I am, Your sincerely, Anne Marie.

HOW TO WORK NON-CO-OPERATION

Perhaps the best way of answering the fears and criticism as to non-co-operation is to elaborate more fully the scheme of non-co-operation. The critics seem to imagine that the organisers propose to give effect to the whole scheme at once. The fact however is that the organisers have fixed definite, progressive four stages. The first is the giving up of titles and resignation of honorary posts. If there is no response or if the response received is not effective, recourse will be had to the second stage. The second stage involves much previous arrangement. Certainly not a single servant will be called out unless he is either capable of supporting himself and his dependents or the Khilafat Committee is able to bear the burden. All the classes of servants will not be called out at once and never will any pressure be put upon a single servant to withdraw himself from the Government service. Nor will a single private employee be touched for the simple reason that the movement is not anti-English. It is not even anti-Government. Co-operation is to be withdrawn because the people must not be party to a wrong--a broken pledge--a violation of deep religious sentiment. Naturally, the movement will receive a check, if there is any undue influence brought to bear upon any Government servant or if any violence is used or countenanced by any member of the Khilafat Committee. The second stage must be entirely successful, if the response is at all on an adequate scale. For no Government--much less the Indian Government--can subsist if the people cease to serve it. The withdrawal therefore of the police and the military--the third stage--is a distant goal. The organisers however wanted to be fair, open and above suspicion. They did not want to keep back from the Government or the public a single step they had in contemplation even as a remote contingency. The fourth, *i.e.,* suspension of taxes is still more remote. The organisers recognise that suspension of general taxation is fraught with the greatest danger. It is likely to bring a sensitive class in conflict with the police. They are therefore not likely to embark upon it, unless they can do so with the assurance that there will be no violence offered by the people.

I admit as I have already done that non-co-operation is not unattended with risk, but the risk of supineness in the face of a grave issue is infinitely greater than the danger of violence ensuing form organizing non-co-operation. To do nothing is to invite violence for a certainty.

It is easy enough to pass resolutions or write articles condemning non-co-operation. But it is no easy task to restrain the fury of a people incensed by a deep sense of wrong. I urge those who talk or work against non-co-operation to descend from their chairs and go down to the people, learn their feelings and write, if they have the heart against non-co-operation. They will find, as I have found that the only way to avoid violence is to enable them to give such expression to their feelings as to compel redress. I have found nothing save non-co-operation. It is logical and harmless. It is the inherent right of a subject to refuse to assist a Government that will not listen to him.

Non-co-operation as a voluntary movement can only succeed, if the feeling is genuine and strong enough to make people suffer to the utmost. If the religious sentiment of the Mahomedans is deeply hurt and if the Hindus entertain neighbourly regard towards their Muslim brethren, they will both count no cost too great for achieving the end. Non-co-operation will not only be an effective remedy but will also be an effective test of the sincerity of the Muslim claim and the Hindu profession of friendship.

There is however one formidable argument urged by friends against my joining the Khilafat movement. They say that it ill-becomes me, a friend of the English and an admirer of the British constitution, to join hands with those who are to-day filled with nothing but ill-will against the English. I am sorry to have to confess that the ordinary Mahomedan entertains to-day no affection for Englishmen. He considers, not without some cause, that they have not played the game. But if I am friendly towards Englishmen, I am no less so towards my countrymen, the Mahomedans. And as such they have a greater claim upon my attention than Englishmen. My personal religion however enables me to serve my countrymen without hurting Englishmen or for that matter anybody else. What I am not prepared to do to my blood-brother I would not do to an Englishman, I would not injure him to gain a kingdom. But I would withdraw co-operation from him if it becomes necessary as I had withdrawn from my own brother (now deceased) when it became necessary. I serve the Empire by refusing to partake in its wrong. William Stead offered public prayers for British reverses at the time of the Boer war because he considered that the nation to which he belonged was engaged in an unrighteous war. The present Prime Minister risked his life in opposing that war and did everything he could to obstruct his own Government in its prosecution. And to-day if I have thrown in my lot with the Mahomedans, a large number of whom, bear no friendly feelings towards the British, I have done so frankly as a friend of the British and with the object of gaining justice and of thereby showing the capacity of the British constitution to respond to every honest determination when it is coupled with suffering, I hope by my 'alliance' with the Mahomedans to achieve a threefold end--to obtain justice in the face of odds with the method of Satyagrah and to show its efficacy over all other methods, to secure Mahomedan friendship for the Hindus and thereby internal peace also, and last but not least to transform ill-will into affection for the British and their constitution which in spite of the imperfections weathered many a storm. I may fail in achieving any of the ends. I can but attempt. God alone can grant success. It will not be denied that the ends are all worthy. I invite Hindus and Englishman to join me in a full-hearted manner in shouldering the burden the Mahomedans of India are carrying. Theirs is admittedly a just fight. The Viceroy, the Secretary of State, the Maharaja of Bikuner and Lord Sinha have testified to it. Time has arrived to make good the testimony. People with a just cause are never satisfied with a mere protest. They have been known to die for it. Are a high-spirited people like the Mahomedans expected to do less?

SPEECH AT MADRAS

> Addressing a huge concourse of people of the city of Madras Hindus and Mahomedans numbering over 50,000, assembled on the South Beach opposite to the Presidency College, Madras, on the 12th August 1920, Mahatma Gandhi spoke as follows:--

Mr. Chairman and Friends,--Like last year, I have to ask your forgiveness that I should have to speak being seated. Whilst my voice has become stronger than it was last year, my body is still weak; and if I were to attempt to speak to you standing, I could not hold on for very many minutes before the whole frame would shake. I hope, therefore, that you will grant me permission to speak seated. I have sat here to address you on a most important question, probably a question whose importance we have not measured up to now.

LOKAMANYA TILAK

But before I approach that question on this dear old beach of Madras, you will expect me--you will want me--to offer my tribute to the great departed, Lokamanya Tilak Maharaj (loud and prolonged cheers). I would ask this great assembly to listen to me in silence. I have come to make an appeal to your hearts and to your reason and I could not do so unless you were prepared to listen to whatever I have to say in absolute silence. I wish to offer my tribute to the departed patriot and I think that I cannot do better than say that his death, as his life, has poured new vigour into the country. If you were present as I was present at that great funeral procession, you would realise with me the meaning of my words. Mr. Tilak lived for his country. The inspiration of his life was freedom for his country which he called Swaraj the inspiration of his death-bed was also freedom for his country. And it was that which gave him such marvellous hold upon his countrymen; it was that which commanded the adoration not of a few chosen Indians belonging to the upper strata of society but of millions of his countrymen. His life was one long sustained piece of self-sacrifice. He began that life of discipline and self-sacrifice in 1879 and he continued that life up to the end of his day, and that was the secret of his hold upon his country. He not only knew what he wanted for his country but also how to live for his country and how to die for his country. I hope then that whatever I say this evening to this vast mass of people, will bear fruit in that same sacrifice for which the life of Lokamanya Tilak Maharaj stands. His life, if it teaches us anything whatsoever, teaches one supreme lesson: that if we want to do anything whatsoever for our country we can do so not by speeches, however grand, eloquent and convincing they may be, but only by sacrifice at the back of every act of our life. I have come to ask everyone of you whether you are ready and willing to give sufficiently for your country's sake for country's honour and for religion. I have boundless faith in you, the citizens of Madras, and the people of this great presidency, a faith which I began to cultivate in the year 1903 when I first made acquaintance with the Tamil labourers in South Africa; and I hope that in these hours of our trial, this province will not be second to any other in India, and that it will lead in this spirit of self-sacrifice and will translate every word into action.

NEED FOR NON-CO-OPERATION

What is this non-co-operation, about which you have heard so much, and why do we want to offer this non-co-operation? I wish to go for the time being into the why. Here are two things before this country: the first and the foremost is the Khilafat question. On this the heart of the Mussalmans of India has become lascerated. British pledges given after the greatest deliberation by the Prime Minister of England in the name of the English nation, have been dragged into the mire. The promises given to Moslem India on the strength of which, the consideration that was expected by the British nation was exacted, have been broken, and the great religion of Islam has been placed in danger. The Mussalmans hold--and I venture to think they rightly hold--that so long as British promises remain unfulfilled, so long is it impossible for them to tender whole-hearted fealty and loyalty to the British connection; and if it is to be a choice for a devout Mussalman between loyalty to the British connection and loyalty to his Code and Prophet, he will not require a second to make his choice,--and he has declared his choice. The Mussalmans say frankly openly and honourably to the whole world that if the British Ministers and the British nation do not fulfil the pledges given to them and do not wish to regard with respect the sentiments of 70 millions of the inhabitants of India who profess the faith of Islam, it will be impossible for them to retain Islamic loyalty. It is a question, then for the rest of the Indian population to consider whether they want to perform a neighbourly duty by their Mussalman countrymen, and if they do, they have an opportunity of a lifetime which will not occur for another hundred years, to show their good-will, fellowship and friendship and to prove what they have been saying for all these long years that the Mussalman is the brother of the Hindu. If the Hindu regards that before the connection with the British nation comes his natural connection with his Moslem brother, then I say to you that if you find that the Moslem claim is just, that it is based upon real sentiment, and that at its back ground is this great religious feeling, you cannot do otherwise than help the Mussalman through and through, so long as their cause remains just, and the means for attaining the end remains equally just, honourable and free from harm to India. These are the plain conditions which the Indian Mussalmans have accepted; and it was when they saw that they could accept the proferred aid of the Hindus, that they could always justify the cause and the means before the whole world, that they decided to accept the proferred hand of fellowship. It is then for the Hindus and Mahomedans to offer a united front to the whole of the Christian powers of Europe and tell them that weak as India is, India has still got the capacity of preserving her self-respect, she still knows how to die for her religion and for her self-respect.

That is the Khilafat in a nut-shell; but you have also got the Punjab. The Punjab has wounded the heart of India as no other question has for the past century. I do not exclude from my calculation the Mutiny of 1857. Whatever hardships India had to suffer during the Mutiny, the insult that was attempted to be offered to her during the passage of the Rowlatt legislation and that which was offered after its passage were unparalleled in Indian history. It is because you want justice from the British nation in connection with the Punjab atrocities: you have to devise, ways and means as to how you can get this justice. The House of Commons, the House of Lords, Mr. Montagu, the Viceroy of India, everyone of them know what the feeling of India is on this Khilafat question and on that of the Punjab; the debates in both the Houses of Parliament, the action of Mr. Montagu and that of the Viceroy have demonstrated to you completely that they are not willing to give the justice which is India's due and which she demands. I suggest that our leaders have got to find a way out of this great difficulty and unless we have made ourselves even with the British rulers in India and unless we have gained a measure of self-respect at the hands of the British rulers in India, no connection, and no friendly intercourse is possible between them and ourselves. I, therefore, venture to suggest this beautiful and unanswerable method of non-co-operation.

IS IT UNCONSTITUTIONAL?

I have been told that non-co-operation is unconstitutional. I venture to deny that it is unconstitutional. On the contrary, I hold that non-co-operation is a just and religious doctrine; it is the inherent right of every human being and it is perfectly constitutional. A great lover of the British Empire has said that under the British constitution even a successful rebellion is perfectly constitutional and he quotes historical instances, which I cannot deny, in support of his claim. I do not claim any constitutionality for a rebellion successful or otherwise, so long as that rebellion means in the ordinary sense of the term, what it does mean namely wresting justice by violent means. On the contrary, I have said it repeatedly to my countrymen that violence whatever end it may serve in Europe, will never serve us in India. My brother and friend Shaukat Ali believes in methods of violence; and if it was in his power to draw the sword against the British Empire, I know that he has got the courage of a man and he has got also the wisdom to see that he should offer that battle to the British Empire. But because he recognises as a true soldier that means of violence are not open to India, he sides with me accepting my humble assistance and pledges his word that so long as I am with him and so long as he believes in the doctrine, so long will he not harbour even the idea of violence against any single Englishman or any single man on earth. I am here to tell you that he has been as true as his word and has kept it religiously. I am here to bear witness that he has been following out this plan of non-violent Non-co-operation to the very letter and I am asking India to follow this non-violent non-co-operation. I tell you that there is not a better soldier living in our ranks in British India than Shaukat Ali. When the time for the drawing of the sword comes, if it ever comes, you will find him drawing that sword and you will find me retiring to the jungles of Hindustan. As soon as India accepts the doctrine of the sword, my life as an Indian is finished. It is because I believe in a mission special to India and it is because I believe that the ancients of India after centuries of experience have found out that the true thing for any human being on earth is not justice based on violence but justice based on sacrifice of self, justice based on Yagna and Kurbani,--I cling to that doctrine and I shall cling to it for ever,--it is for that reason I tell you that whilst my friend believes also in the doctrine of violence and has adopted the doctrine of non-violence as a weapon of the weak, I believe in the doctrine of non-violence as a weapon of the strongest. I believe that a man is the strongest soldier for daring to die unarmed with his breast bare before the enemy. So much for the non-violent part of non-co-operation. I therefore, venture to suggest to my learned countrymen that so long as the doctrine of non-co-operation remains non-violent, so long there is nothing unconstitutional in that doctrine.

I ask further, is it unconstitutional for me to say to the British Government 'I refuse to serve you?' Is it unconstitutional for our worthy Chairman to return with every respect all the titles that he has ever held from the Government? Is it unconstitutional for any parent to withdraw his children from a Government or aided school? Is it unconstitutional for a lawyer to say 'I shall no longer support the arm of the law so long as that arm of law is used not to raise me but to debase me'? Is it unconstitutional for a civil servant or for a judge to say, 'I refuse to serve a Government which does not wish to respect the wishes of the whole people?' I ask, is it unconstitutional for a policeman or for a soldier to tender his resignation when he knows that he is called to serve a Government which traduces his own countrymen? Is it unconstitutional for me to go to the 'krishan,' to the agriculturist, and say to him 'it is not wise for you to pay any taxes if these taxes are used by the Government not to raise you but to weaken you?' I hold and I venture to submit, that there is nothing unconstitutional in it. What is more, I have done every one of these things in my life and nobody has questioned the constitutional character of it. I was in Kaira working in the midst of 7 lakhs of agriculturists. They had all suspended the payment of taxes and the whole of India was at one with me. Nobody considered that it was unconstitutional. I submit that in the whole plan of non-co-operation, there is nothing unconstitutional. But I do venture to suggest that it will be highly unconstitutional in the midst of this unconstitutional Government,--in the midst of a nation which has built up its magnificent constitution,--for the people of India to become weak and to crawl on their belly--it will be highly unconstitutional for the people of India to pocket every insult that is offered to them; it is highly unconstitutional for the 70 millions of Mohamedans of India to submit to a violent wrong done to their religion; it is highly unconstitutional for the whole of India to sit still and co-operate with an unjust Government which has trodden under its feet the honour of the Punjab. I say to my countrymen so long as you have a sense of honour and so long as you wish to remain the descendants and defenders of the noble traditions that have been handed to you for generations after generations, it is unconstitutional for you not to non-co-operate and unconstitutional for you to co-operate with a Government which has become so unjust as our Government has become. I am not anti-English; I am not anti-British; I am not anti any Government; but I am anti-untruth--anti-humbug and anti-injustice. So long as the Government spells injustice, it may regard me as its enemy, implacable enemy. I had hoped at the Congress at Amritsar--I am speaking God's truth before you--when I pleaded on bended knees before some of you for co-operation with the Government. I had full hope that the British ministers who are wise, as a rule, would placate the Mussalman sentiment that they would do full justice in the matter of the Punjab atrocities; and therefore, I said:--let us return good-will to the hand of fellowship that has been extended to us, which I then believed was extended to us through the Royal Proclamation. It was on that account that I pleaded for co-operation. But to-day that faith having gone and obliterated by the acts of the British ministers, I am here to plead not for futile obstruction in the Legislative council but for real substantial non-co-operation which would paralyse the mightiest Government on earth. That is what I stand for to-day. Until we have wrung justice, and until we have wrung our self-respect from unwilling hands and from unwilling pens there can be no co-operation. Our Shastras say and I say so with the greatest deference to all the greatest religious preceptors of India but without fear of contradiction, that our Shastras teach us that there shall be no co-operation between injustice and justice, between an unjust man and a justice-loving man, between truth and untruth. Co-operation is a duty only so long as Government protects your honour, and non-co-operation is an equal duty when the Government instead of protecting robs you of your honour. That is the doctrine of non-co-operation.

NON-CO-OPERATION AND THE SPECIAL CONGRESS

I have been told that I should have waited for the declaration of the special Congress which is the mouth piece of the whole nation. I know that it is the mouthpiece of the whole nation. If it was for me, individual Gandhi, to wait, I would have waited for eternity. But I had in my hands a sacred trust. I was advising my Mussalman countrymen and for the time being I hold their honour in my hands. I dare not ask them to wait for any verdict but the verdict of their own Conscience. Do you suppose that Mussalmans can eat their own words, can withdraw from the honourable position they have taken up? If perchance--and God forbid that it should happen--the Special Congress decides against them, I would still advise my countrymen the Mussalmans to stand single handed and fight rather than yield to the attempted dishonour to their religion. It is therefore given to the Mussalmans to go to the Congress on bended knees and plead for support. But support or no support, it was not possible for them to wait for the Congress to give them the lead. They had to choose between futile violence, drawing of the naked sword and peaceful non-violent but effective non-co-operation, and they have made their choice. I venture further to say to you that if there is any body of men who feel as I do, the sacred character of non-co-operation, it is for you and me not to wait for the Congress but to act and to make it impossible for the Congress to give any other verdict. After all what is the Congress? The Congress is the collected voice of individuals who form it, and if the individuals go to the Congress with a united voice, that will be the verdict you will gain from the Congress. But if we go to the Congress with no opinion because we have none or because we are afraid to express it, then naturally we wait the verdict of the Congress. To those who are unable to make up their mind I say by all means wait. But for those who have seen the clear light as they see the lights in front of them, for them to wait is a sin. The Congress does not expect you to wait but it expects you to act so that the Congress can gauge properly the national feeling. So much for the Congress.

BOYCOTT OF THE COUNCILS

Among the details of non-co-operation I have placed in the foremost rank the boycott of the councils. Friends have quarrelled with me for the use of the word boycott, because I have disapproved--as I disapprove even now--boycott of British goods or any goods for that matter. But there, boycott has its own meaning and here boycott has its own meaning. I not only do not disapprove but approve of the boycott of the councils that are going to be formed next year. And why do I do it? The people--the masses,--require from us, the leaders, a clear lead. They do not want any equivocation from us. The suggestion that we should seek election and then refuse to take the oath of allegiance, would only make the nation distrust the leaders. It is not a clear lead to the nation. So I say to you, my countrymen, not to fall into this trap. We shall sell our country by adopting the method of seeking election and then not taking the oath of allegiance. We may find it difficult, and I frankly confess to you that I have not that trust in so many Indians making that declaration and standing by it. To-day I suggest to those who honestly hold the view--

viz

. that we should seek election and then refuse to take the oath of allegiance--I suggest to them that they will fall into a trap which they are preparing for themselves and for the nation. That is my view. I hold that if we want to give the nation the clearest possible lead, and if we want not to play with this great nation we must make it clear to this nation that we cannot take any favours, no matter how great they may be so long as those favours are accompanied by an injustice a double wrong, done to India not yet redressed. The first indispensable thing before we can receive any favours from them is that they should redress this double wrong. There is a Greek proverb which used to say "Beware of the Greek but especially beware of them when they bring gifts to you." To-day from those ministers who are bent upon perpetuating the wrong to Islam and to the Punjab, I say we cannot accept gifts but we should be doubly careful lest we may not fall into the trap that they may have devised. I therefore suggest that we must not coquet with the council and must not have anything whatsoever to do with them. I am told that if we, who represent the national sentiment do not seek election, the Moderates who do not represent that sentiment will. I do not agree. I do not know what the Moderates represent and I do not know what the Nationalists represent. I know that there are good sheep and black sheep amongst the Moderates. I know that there are good sheep and black sheep amongst the Nationalists. I know that many Moderates hold honestly the view that it is a sin to resort to non-co-operation. I respectfully agree to differ from them. I do say to them also that they will fall into a trap which they will have devised if they seek election. But that does not affect my situation. If I feel in my heart of hearts that I ought not to go to the councils I ought at least to abide by this decision and it does not matter if ninety-nine other countrymen seek election. That is the only way in which public work can be done, and public opinion can be built. That is the only way in which reforms can be achieved and religion can be conserved. If it is a question of religious honour, whether I am one or among many I must stand upon my doctrine. Even if I should die in the attempt, it is worth dying for, than that I should live and deny my own doctrine. I suggest that it will be wrong on the part of any one to seek election to these Councils. If once we feel that we cannot co-operate with this Government, we have to commence from the top. We are the natural leaders of the people and we have acquired the right and the power to go to the nation and speak to it with the voice of non-co-operation. I therefore do suggest that it is inconsistent with non-co-operation to seek election to the Councils on any terms whatsoever.

LAWYERS AND NON-CO-OPERATION

I have suggested another difficult matter,

viz.

, that the lawyers should suspend their practice. How should I do otherwise knowing so well how the Government had always been able to retain this power through the instrumentality of lawyers. It is perfectly true that it is the lawyers of to-day who are leading us, who are fighting the country's battles, but when it comes to a matter of action against the

Government, when it comes to a matter of paralysing the activity of the Government I know that the Government always look to the lawyers, however fine fighters they may have been to preserve their dignity and their self-respect. I therefore suggest to my lawyer friends that it is their duty to suspend their practice and to show to the Government that they will no longer retain their offices, because lawyers are considered to be honorary officers of the courts and therefore subject to their disciplinary jurisdiction. They must no longer retain these honorary offices if they want to withdraw on operation from Government. But what will happen to law and order? We shall evolve law and order through the instrumentality of these very lawyers. We shall promote arbitration courts and dispense justice, pure, simple home-made justice, swadeshi justice to our countrymen. That is what suspension of practice means.

PARENTS AND NON-CO-OPERATION

I have suggested yet another difficulty--to withdraw our children from the Government schools and to ask collegiate students to withdraw from the College and to empty Government aided schools. How could I do otherwise? I want to gauge the national sentiment. I want to know whether the Mahomodans feel deeply. If they feel deeply they will understand in the twinkling of an eye, that it is not right for them to receive schooling from a Government in which they have lost all faith; and which they do not trust at all. How can I, if I do not want to help this Government, receive any help from that Government. I think that the schools and colleges are factories for making clerks and Government servants. I would not help this great factory for manufacturing clerks and servants if I want to withdraw co-operation from that Government. Look at it from any point of view you like. It is not possible for you to send your children to the schools and still believe in the doctrine of non-co-operation.

THE DUTY OF TITLE HOLDERS

I have gone further. I have suggested that our title holders should give up their titles. How can they hold on to the titles and honour bestowed by the Government? They were at one time badges of honours when we believed that national honour was safe in their hands. But now they are no longer badges of honour but badges of dishonour and disgrace when we really believe that we cannot get justice from this Government. Every title holder holds his titles and honours as trustee for the nation and in this first step in the withdrawal of co-operation from the Government they should surrender their titles without a moment's consideration. I suggest to my Mahomedan countrymen that if they fail in this primary duty they will certainly fail in non-co-operation unless the masses themselves reject the classes and take up non-co-operation in their own hands and are able to fight that battle even as the men of the French Revolution were able to take the reins of Government in their own hands leaving aside the leaders and marched to the banner of victory. I want no revolution. I want ordered progress. I want no disordered order. I want no chaos. I want real order to be evolved out of this chaos which is misrepresented to me as order. If it is order established by a tyrant in order to get hold of the tyrannical reins of Government I say that it is no order for me but it is disorder. I want to evolve justice out of this injustice. Therefore, I suggest to you the passive non-co-operation. If we would only realise the secret of this peaceful and infallible doctrine you will know and you will find that you will not want to use even an angry word when they lift the sword at you and you will not want even to lift your little finger, let alone a stick or a sword.

NON-CO-OPERATION--SERVICE TO THE EMPIRE

You may consider that I have spoken these words in anger because I have considered the ways of this Government immoral, unjust, debasing and untruthful. I use these adjectives with the greatest deliberation. I have used them for my own true brother with whom I was engaged in battle of non-co-operation for full 13 years and although the ashes cover the remains of my brother I tell you that I used to tell him that he was unjust when his plans were based upon immoral foundation. I used to tell him that he did not stand for truth. There was no anger in me, I told him this home truth because I loved him. In the same manner, I tell the British people that I love them, and that I want their association but I want that association on conditions well defined. I want my self-respect and I want my absolute equality with them. If I cannot gain that equality from the British people, I do not want that British connection. If I have to let the British people go and import temporary disorder and dislocation of national business, I will favour that disorder and dislocation than that I should have injustice from the hands of a great nation such as the British nation. You will find that by the time the whole chapter is closed that the successors of Mr. Montagu will give me the credit for having rendered the most distinguished service that I have yet rendered to the Empire, in having offered this non-co-operation and in having suggest the boycott, not of His Royal Highness the principle of Wales, but of boycott of a visit engineered by Government in order to tighten its hold on the national neck. I will not allow it even if I stand alone, if I cannot persuade this nation not to welcome that visit but will boycott that visit with all the power at my command. It is for that reason I stand before you and implore you to offer this religious battle, but it is not a battle offered to you by a visionary or a saint. I deny being a visionary. I do not accept the claim of saintliness. I am of the earth, earthy, a common gardener man as much as any one of you, probably much more than you are. I am prone to as many weaknesses as you are. But I have seen the world. I have lived in the world with my eyes open. I have gone through the most fiery ordeals that have fallen to the lot of man. I have gone through this discipline. I have understood the secret of my own sacred Hinduism. I have learnt the lesson that non-co-operation is the duty not merely of the saint but it is the duty of every ordinary citizen, who not know much, not caring to know much but wants to perform his ordinary household functions. The people of Europe touch even their masses, the poor people the doctrine of the sword. But the Rishis of India, those who have held the tradition of India have preached to the masses of India this doctrine, not of the sword, not of violence but of suffering, of self-suffering. And unless you and I am prepared to go through this primary lesson we are not ready even to offer the sword and that is the lesson my brother Shaukal Ali has imbibed to teach and that is why he to-day accepts my advice tendered to him in all prayerfulness and in all humility and says 'long live non-co-operation.' Please remember that even in England the little children were withdrawn from the schools; and colleges in Cambridge and Oxford were closed. Lawyers had left their desks and were fighting in the trenches. I do not present to you the trenches but I do ask you to go through the sacrifice that the men, women and the brave lads of England went through. Remember that you are offering battle to a nation which is saturated with their spirit of sacrifice whenever the occasion arises. Remember that the little band of Boers offered stubborn resistance to a mighty nation. But their lawyers had left their desks. Their mothers had withdrawn their children from the schools and colleges and the children had become the volunteers of the nation, I have seen them with these naked eyes of mine. I am asking my countrymen in India to follow no other gospel than the gospel of self-sacrifice which precedes every battle. Whether you belong to the school of violence or non-violence you will still have to go through the fire of sacrifice, and of discipline. May God grant you, may God grant our leaders the wisdom, the courage and the true knowledge to lead the nation to its cherished goal. May God grant the people of India the right path, the true vision and the ability and the courage to follow this path, difficult and yet easy, of sacrifice.

SPEECH AT TRICHINOPOLY

Mahatma Gandhi made the following speech at Trichinopoly on the 18th August 1920:--

I thank you on behalf of my brother Shaukat Ali and myself for the magnificent reception that the citizens of Trichinopoly have given to us. I thank you also for the many addresses that you have been good enough to present to us, but I must come to business.

It is a great pleasure to me to renew your acquaintance for reasons that I need not give you. I expect great things from Trichinopoly, Madura and a few places I could name. I take it that you have read my address on the Madras Beach on non-co-operation. Without taking up your time in this great assembly, I wish to deal with one or two matters that arise out of Mr. S. Kasturiranga Iyongar's speech. He says in effect that I should have waited for the Congress mandate on Non-co-operation. That was impossible, because the Mussulmans had and still have a duty, irrespective of the Hindus, to perform in reference to their own religion. It was impossible for them to wait for any mandate save the mandate of their own religion in a matter that vitally concerned the honour of Islam. It is therefore possible for them only to go to the Congress on bended knees with a clear cut programme of their own and ask the Congress to pronounce its blessings upon that programme and if they are not so fortunate as to secure the blessings of the National Assembly without meaning any disrespect to that assembly, it is their bounden duty to go on with their programme, and so it is the duty of every Hindu who considers his Mussalman brother as a brother who has a just cause which he wishes to vindicate, to throw in his lot with his Mussalman brother. Our leader does not quarrel with the principle of non-co-operation by itself, but he objects to the three principal details of non-co-operation.

COUNCIL ELECTIONS

He considers that it is our duty to seek election to the Councils and fight our battle on the floor of the Council hall. I do not deny the possibility of a fight and a royal fight on the Council floor. We have done it for the last 35 years, but I venture to suggest to you and to him, with all due respect, that it is not non-co-operation and it is not half as successful as non-co-operation can be. You cannot go to a class of people with a view to convince them by any fight--call it even obstruction--who have got a settled conviction and a settled policy to follow. It is in medical language an incompatible mixture out of which you can gain nothing, but if you totally boycott the Council, you create a public opinion in the country with reference to the Khilafat wrong and the Punjab wrong which will become totally irresistible. The first advantage of going to the Councils must be good-will on the part of the rulers. It is absolutely lacking. In the place of good-will you have got nothing but injustice but I must move on.

LAWYERS' PRACTICE

I come now to the second objection of Mr. Kasturiranga Iyengar with reference to the suspension by lawyers of their practice. Milk is good in itself but it comes absolutely poisonous immediately a little bit of arsenic is added to it. Law courts are similarly good when justice is distilled through them on behalf of a Sovereign power which wants to do justice to its people. Law courts are one of the greatest symbols of power and in the battle of non-co-operation, you may not leave law courts untouched and claim to offer non-co-operation, but if you will read that objection carefully, you will find in that objection the great fear that the lawyers will not respond to the call that the country makes upon them, and it is just there that the beauty of non-co-operation comes in. If one lawyer alone suspends practice, it is so much to the good of the country and so if we are sure to deprive the Government of the power that it possess through its law courts, whether one lawyer takes it up or many, we must adopt that step.

GOVERNMENT SCHOOLS

He objects also to the plan of boycotting Government schools. I can only say what I have said with reference to lawyers that if we mean non-co-operation, we may not receive any favours from the Government, no matter how advantageous by themselves they may be. In a great struggle like this, it is not open to us to count how many schools will respond and how many parents will respond and just as a geometrical problem is difficult, because it does not admit of easy proof, so also because a certain stage in national evolution is difficult, you may not avoid that step without making the whole of the evolution a farce.

We have had a great lesson in non-co-operation and co-operation. We had a lesson in non-co-operation when some young men began to fight there and it is a dangerous weapon. I have not the slightest doubt about it. One man with a determined will to non-co-operate can disturb a whole meeting and we had a physical demonstration of it to night but ours is non-violent, non-co-operation in which there can be no mistake whatsoever in the fundamental conditions are observed. If non-co-operation fails, it will not be for want of any inherent strength in it, but it will fall because there is no response to it, or because people have not sufficiently grasped its simple principles. You had also a practical demonstration of co-operation just now;

that heavy chair went over the heads of so many people, because all wanted to lift their little hand to move that chair away from them and so was that heavier dome also removed from our sight by co-operation of man, woman and child. Everybody believes and knows that this Government of our exists only by the co-operation of the people and not by the force of arms it can wield and everyman with a sense of logic will tell you that the converse of that also is equally true that Government cannot stand if this co-operation on which it exists is withdrawn. Difficulties undoubtedly there are, we have hitherto learned how to sacrifice our voice and make speeches. We must also learn to sacrifice ease, money, comfort and that, we may learn form the Englishmen themselves. Every one who has studied English history knows that we are now engaged in a battle with a nation which is capable of great sacrifice and the three hundred millions of India cannot make their mark upon the world, or gain their self-respect without an adequate measure of sacrifice.

BOYCOTT OF BRITISH GOODS

Our friend has suggested the boycott of British or foreign goods. Boycott of all foreign goods is another name for Swadeshi. He thinks that there will be a greater response in the boycott of all foreign goods. With the experience of years behind me and with an intimate knowledge of the mercantile classes, I venture to tell you that boycott of foreign goods, or boycott of merely British goods is more impracticable than any of the stops I have suggested. Whereas in all the steps that I have ventured to suggest there is practically no sacrifice of money involved, in the boycott of British or foreign goods you are inviting your merchant princes to sacrifice their millions. It has got to be done, but it is an exceedingly low process. The same may be said of the steps that I have ventured to suggest, I know, but boycott of goods in conceived as a punishment and the punishment is only effective when it is inflicted. What I have ventured to suggest is not a punishment, but the performance of a sacred duty, a measure of self-denial from ourselves, and therefore it is effective from its very inception when it is undertaken even by one man and a substantial duty performed even by one single man lays the foundation of nations liberty.

CONCLUSION

I am most anxious for my nation, for my Mussalman brethren also, to understand that if they want to vindicate national honour or the honour of Islam, it will be vindicated without a shadow of doubt, not be conceiving a punishment or a series of punishments, but by an adequate measure of self-sacrifice. I wish to speak of all our leaders in terms of the greatest respect, but whatever respect we wish to pay them may not stop or arrest the progress of the country, and I am most anxious that the country at this very critical period of its history should make its choice. The choice clearly does not lie before you and me in wresting by force of arms the sceptre form the British nation, but the choice lies in suffering this double wrong of the Khilafat and the Punjab, in pocketing humiliation and in accepting national emasculation or vindication of India's honour by sacrifice to-day by every man, woman and child and those who feel convinced of the rightness of things, we should make that choice to-night. So, citizens of Trichinopoly, you may not wait for the whole of India but you can enforce the first step of non-co-operation and begin your operations even from to-morrow, if you have not done so already. You can surrender all your titles to-morrow all the lawyers may surrender their practice to-morrow; those who cannot sustain body and soul by any other means can be easily supported by the Khilafat Committee, if they will give their whole time and attention to the work of that Committee and if the layers will kindly do that, you will find that there is no difficulty in settling your disputes by private arbitration. You can nationalise your schools from to-morrow if you have got the will and the determination. It is difficult, I know, when only a few of you think these things. It is as easy as we are sitting here when the whole of this vast audience is of one mind and as it was easy for you to carry that chair so is it easy for you to enforce this programme from to-morrow if you have one will, one determination and love for your country, love for the honour of your country and religion. (Loud and prolonged cheers.)

SPEECH AT CALICUT

Mr. Chairman and friends.--On behalf of my brother Shaukut Ali and myself I wish to thank you most sincerely for the warm welcome you have extended to us. Before I begin to explain the purpose of our mission I have to give you the information that Pir Mahboob Shah who was being tried in Sindh for sedition has been sentenced to two years' simple imprisonment. I do not know exactly what the offence was with which the Pir was charged. I do not know whether the words attributed to him were ever spoken by him. But I do know that the Pirsaheb declined to offer any defence and with perfect resignation he has accepted his penalty. For me it is a matter of sincere pleasure that the Pirsaheb who exercises great influence over his followers has understood the spirit of the struggle upon which we have embarked. It is not by resisting the authority of Government that we expect to succeed in the great task before us. But I do expect that we shall succeed if we understand the spirit of non-co-operation. The Lieutenant-Governor of Burma himself has told us that the British retain their hold on India not by the force of arms but by the force of co-operation of the people. Thus he has given us the remedy for any wrong that the Government may do to the people, whether knowingly or unknowingly. And so long as we co-operate with the Government, so long as we support that Government, we become to that extent sharers in the wrong. I admit that in ordinary circumstances a wise subject will tolerate the wrongs of a Government, but a wise subject never tolerates a wrong that a Government imposes on the declared will of a people. And I venture to submit to this great meeting that the Government of India and the Imperial Government have done a double wrong to India, and if we are a nation of self-respecting people conscious of its dignity, conscious of its right, it is not just and proper that we should stand the double humiliation that the Government has heaped upon us. By shaping and by becoming a predominant partner in the peace terms imposed on the helpless Sultan of Turkey, the Imperial Government have intentionally flouted the cherished sentiment of the Mussalman subjects of the Empire. The present Prime Minister gave a deliberate pledge after consultation with his colleagues when it was necessary for him to conciliate the Mussalmans of India. I claim to have studied this Khilafat question in a special manner. I claim to understand the Mussalman feeling on the Khilafat question and I am here to declare for the tenth time that on the Khilafat matter the Government has wounded the Mussalman sentiment as they had never done before. And I say without fear of contradiction that if the Mussalmans of India had not exercised great self-restraint and if there was not the gospel of non-co-operation preached to them and if they had not accepted it, there would have been bloodshed in India by this time. I am free to confess that spilling of blood would not have availed their cause. But a man who is in a state of rage whose heart has become lacerated does not count the cost of his action. So much for the Khilafat wrong.

I propose to take you for a minute to the Punjab, the northern end of India. And what have both Governments done for the Punjab? I am free to confess again that the crowds in Amritsar went mad for a moment. They were goaded to madness by a wicked administration. But no madness on the part of a people can justify the shedding of innocent blood, and what have they paid for it? I venture to submit that no civilised Government could ever have made the people pay the penalty and retribution that they have paid. Innocent men were tried through mock-tribunals and imprisoned for life. Amnesty granted to them after; I count of no consequence. Innocent, unarmed men, who knew nothing of what was to happen, were butchered in cold blood without the slightest notice. Modesty of women in Manianwalla, women who had done no wrong to any individual, was outraged by insolent officers. I want you to understand what I mean by outrage of their modesty. Their veils were opened with his stick by an officer. Men who were declared to be utterly innocent by the Hunter Committee were made to crawl on their bellies. And all these wrongs totally undeserved remain unavenged. If it was the duty of the Government of India to punish those who were guilty of incendiarism and murder, as I hold it was their duty, it was doubly their duty to punish officers who insulted and oppressed innocent people. But in the face of these official wrongs we have the debate in the house of lords supporting official terrorism, it is this double wrong, the affront to Islam and the injury to the manhood of the Punjab, that we feel bound to wipe out by non-co-operation. We have prayed, petitioned, agitated, we have passed resolutions. Mr. Mahomed Ali supported by his friends is now waiting on the British public. He has pleaded the cause of Islam in a most manful manner, but his pleading has fallen on deaf ears and we have his word for it that whilst France and Italy have shown great sympathy for the cause of Islam, it is the British Ministers who have shown no sympathy. This shows which way the British Ministers and the present holders of office in India mean to deal by the people. There is no goodwill, there is no desire to placate the people of India. The people of India must therefore have a remedy to redress the double wrong. The method of the west is violence. Wherever the people of the west have felt a wrong either justly or unjustly, they have rebelled and shed blood. As I have said in my letter to the Viceroy of India, half of India does not believe in the remedy of violence. The other half is too weak to offer it. But the whole of India is deeply hurt and stirred by this wrong, and it is for that reason that I have suggested to the people of India the remedy of non-co-operation. I consider it perfectly harmless, absolutely constitutional and yet perfectly efficacious. It is a remedy in which, if it is properly adopted, victory is certain, and it is the age-old remedy of self-sacrifice. Are the Mussalmans of India who feel the great wrong done to Islam ready to make an adequate self-sacrifice? All the scriptures of the world teach us that there can be no compromise between justice and injustice. Co-operation on the part of a justice-loving man with an unjust man is a crime. And if we desire to compel this great Government to the will of the people, as we must, we must adopt this great remedy of non-co-operation. And if the Mussalmans of India offer non-co-operation to Government in order to secure justice in the Khilafat matter, I believe it is duty of the Hindus to help them so long as their moans are just. I consider the eternal friendship between the Hindus and Mussalmans is more important than the British connection. I would prefer any day anarchy and chaos in India to an armed peace brought about by the bayonet between the Hindus and Mussalmans. I have therefore ventured to suggest to my Hindu brethren that if they wanted to live at peace with Mussalmans, there is an opportunity which is not going to recur for the next hundred years. And I venture to assure you that if the Government of India and the Imperial Government come to know that there is a determination on the part of the people to redress this double wrong they would not hesitate to do what is needed. But in the Mussalmans of India will have to take the lead in the matter. You will have to commence the first stage of non-co-operation in right earnest. And if you may not help this Government, you may not receive help from it. Titles which were the other day titles of honour are to-day in my opinion badges of our disgrace. We must therefore surrender all titles of honour, all honorary offices. It will constitute an emphatic demonstration of the disapproval by the leaders of the people of the acts of the Government. Lawyers must suspend their practice and must resist the power of the Government which has chosen to flout public opinion. Nor may we receive instruction from schools controlled by Government and aided by it. Emptying of the schools will constitute a demonstration of the will of the middle class of India. It is far better for the nation even to neglect the literary instruction of the children than to co-operate with a Government that has striven to maintain an injustice and untruth on the Khilafat and Punjab matters. Similarly have I ventured to suggest a complete boycott of reformed councils. That will be an emphatic declaration of the part of the representatives of the people that they do not desire to associate with the Government so long as the two wrongs continue. We must equally decline to offer ourselves as recruits for the police or the military. It is impossible for us to go to Mesopotamia or to offer to police that country or to offer military assistance and to help the Government in that blood guiltiness. The last plank in the first stage is Swadeshi. Swadeshi is intended not so much to bring pressure upon the Government as to demonstrate the capacity for sacrifice on the part of the men and women of India. When one-fourth of India has its religion at stake and when the whole of India has its honour at stake, we can be in no mood to bedeck ourselves with French calico or silks from Japan. We must resolve to be satisfied with cloth woven by the humble weavers of India in their own cottages out of yarn spun by their sisters in their own homes. When a hundred years ago our tastes were not debased and we were not lured by all the fineries from the foreign countries, we were satisfied with the cloth produced by the men and women in India, and if I could but in a moment revolutionize the tastes of India and make it return to its original simplicity, I assure you that the Gods would descent to rejoice at the great act of renunciation. That is the first stage in non-co-operation. I hope it is as easy for you as it is easy for me to see that if India is capable of taking the first step in anything like a full measure that step will bring the redress we want. I therefore do not intend to take you to the other stages of non-co-operation. I would like you to rivet your attention upon the plans in the first stage. You will have noticed that but two things are necessary in going through the first stage: (1) Prefect spirit of non-violence is indispensable for non-co-operation, (2) only a little self-sacrifice, I pray to God that He will give the people of India sufficient courage and wisdom and patience to go through this experiment of non-co-operation. I think you for the great reception that you have given us. And I also thank you for the great patience and exemplary silence with which you have listened to my remarks.

August 1920.

SPEECH AT MANGALORE

Mr. Chairman and friends,--To my brother Shaukat Ali and me it was a pleasure to go through this beautiful garden of India. The great reception that you gave us this afternoon, and this great assembly are most welcome to us, if they are a demonstration of your sympathy with the cause which you have the honour to represent. I assure you that we have not undertaken this incessant travelling in order to have receptions and addresses, no matter how cordial they may be. But we have undertaken this travelling throughout the length and breadth of this dear Motherland to place before you the position that faces us to-day. It is our privilege, as it is our duty, to place that position before the country and let her make the choice.

Throughout our tour we have received many addresses, but in my humble opinion no address was more truly worded than the address that was presented to us at Kasargod. It addressed both of us as 'dear revered brothers.' I am unable to accept the second adjective 'revered.' The word 'dear' is dear to me I must confess. But dearer than that is the expression 'brothers.' The signatories to that address recognized the true significance of this travel. No blood brothers can possibly be more intimately related, can possibly be more united in one purpose, one aim than my brother Shaukat Ali and I. And I considered it a proud privilege and honour to be addressed as blood brother to Shaukat Ali. The contents of that address were as equally significant. It stated that in our united work was represented the essence of the unity between the Mussalmans and Hindus in India. If we two cannot represent that very desirable unity, if we two cannot cement the relation between the two communities, I do not know who can. Then without any rhetoric and without any flowery language the address went on to describe the inwardness of the Punjab and the Khilafat struggle; and then in simple and beautiful language it described the spiritual significance of Satyagrah and Non-co-operation. This was followed by a frank and simple promise. Although the signatories to the address realised the momentous nature of the struggle on which we have embarked, and although they sympathise with the struggle with their whole heart, they wound up by saying that even if they could not follow non-co-operation in all its details, they would do as much as they could to help the struggle. And lastly, in eloquent, and true language, they said 'if we cannot rise equal to the occasion it will not be due to want of effort but to want of ability.' I can desire no better address, no better promise, and if you, the citizens of Mangalore, can come up to the level of the signatories, and give us just the assurance that you consider the struggle to be right and that it commands your entire approval, I am certain you will make all sacrifice that lies in your power. For we are face to face with a peril greater than plagues, greater than influenza, greater than earthquakes and mighty floods, which sometimes overwhelm this land. These physical calamities can rob us of so many Indian bodies. But the calamity that has at the present moment overtaken India touches the religious honour of a fourth of her children and the self-respect of the whole nation. The Khilafat wrong affects the Mussalmans of India, and the Punjab calamity very nearly overwhelms the manhood of India. Shall we in the face of this danger be weak or rise to our full height. The remedy for both the wrongs is the spiritual solvent of non-co-operation. I call it a spiritual weapon, because it demands discipline and sacrifice from us. It demands sacrifice from every individual irrespective of the rest. And the promise that is behind this performance of duty, the promise given by every religion that I have studied is sure and certain. It is that there is no spotless sacrifice that has been yet offered on earth, which has not carried with it its absolute adequate reward. It is a spiritual weapon, because it waits for no mandate from anybody except one's own conscience. It is a spiritual weapon, because it brings out the best in the nation and it absolutely satisfies individual honour if a single individual takes it, and it will satisfy national honour if the whole nation takes it up. And therefore it is that I have called non-co-operation in opposition to the opinion of many of my distinguished countrymen and leaders--a weapon that is infallible and absolutely practicable. It is infallible and practicable, because it satisfies the demands of individual conscience. God above cannot, will not expect Maulana Shaukat Ali to do more than he has been doing, for he has surrendered and placed at the disposal of God whom he believes to be the Almighty ruler of everyone, he has delivered all in the service of God. And we stand before the citizens of Mangalore and ask them to make their choice either to accept this precious gift that we lay at their feet or to reject it. And after having listened to my message if you come to the come to the conclusion that you have no other remedy than non-co-operation for the conservation of Islam and the honour of India, you will accept that remedy. I ask you not to be confused by so many bewildering issues that are placed before you, nor to be shaken from your purpose because you see divided counsels amongst your leaders. This is one of the necessary limitations of any spiritual or any other struggle that has ever been fought on this earth. It is because it comes so suddenly that it confuses the mind if the heart is not tuned properly. And we would be perfect human beings on this earth if in all of us was found absolutely perfect correspondence between the mind and the heart. But those of you who have been following the newspaper controversy, will find that no matter what division of opinion exists amongst our journals and leaders there is unanimity that the remedy is efficacious if it can be kept free from violence, and if it is adopted on a large scale. I admit the difficulty the virtue however lies in surmounting it. We cannot possibly combine violence with a spiritual weapon like non-co-operation. We do not offer spotless sacrifice if we take the lives of others in offering our own. Absolute freedom from violence is therefore it condition precedent to non-co-operation. But I have faith in my country to know that when it has assimilated the principle of the doctrine In the fullest extent, it will respond to it. And in no case will India make any headway whatsoever until she has learnt the lesson of self-sacrifice. Even if this country were to take up the doctrine of the sword, which God forbid, it will have to learn the lesson of self-sacrifice. The second difficulty suggested is the want of solidarity of the nation. I accept it too. But that difficulty I have already answered by saying that it is a remedy that can be taken up by individuals for individual and by the nation for national satisfaction; and therefore even if the whole nation does not take up non-co-operation, the individual successes, which may be obtained by individuals taking up non-co-operation will stand to their own credit as of the nation to which they belong.

The first stage in my humble opinion is incredibly easy inasmuch as it does not involve any very great sacrifice. If your Khan bahadurs and other title-holders were to renounce their titles I venture to submit that whilst the renunciation will stand to the credit and honour of the nation it will involve a little or no sacrifice. On the contrary, they will not only have surrendered no earthly riches but they will have gained the applause of the nation. Let us see what it means, this first step. The able editor of *Hindu*, Mr. Kastariranga Iyengar, and almost every journalist in the country are agreed that the renunciation of titles is a necessary and a desirable step. And if these chosen people of the Government were without exception to surrender their titles to Government giving notice that the heart of India is doubly wounded in that the honour of India and of muslim religion is at stake and that therefore they can no longer retain their titles, I venture to suggest, that this their step which costs not a single penny either to them or to the nation will be an effective demonstration of the national will.

Take the second step or the second item of non-co-operation. I know there is strong opposition to the boycott of councils. The opposition when you begin to analyse it means not that the step is faulty or that it is not likely to succeed, but it is due to the belief that the whole country will not respond to it and that the Moderates will steal into the councils. I ask the citizens of Mangalore to dispel that fear from your hearts. United the voters of Mangalore can make it impossible for either a moderate or an extremist or any other form of leader to enter the councils as your representative. This step involves no sacrifice of money, no sacrifice of honour but the gaining of prestige for the whole nation. And I venture to suggest to you that this one step alone if it is taken with any degree of unanimity even by the extremists can bring about the desired relief, but if all do not respond the individual need not be afraid. He at least will have laid the foundation for true self progress, let him have the comfort that he at least has washed his hands clean of the guilt of the Government.

Then I come to the members of the profession which one time I used to carry on. I have ventured to ask the lawyers of India to suspend their practice and withdraw their support from a Government which no longer stands for justice, pure and unadulterated, for the nation. And the step is good for the individual lawyer who takes it and is good for the nation if all the lawyers take it.

And so for the Government and the Government aided schools, I must confess that I cannot reconcile my conscience to my children going to Government schools and to the programme of non-co-operation is intended to withdraw all support from Government, and to decline all help from it.

I will not tax your patience by taking you through the other items of non-co-operation important as they are. But I have ventured to place before you four very important and forcible steps any one of which if fully taken up contains in it possibilities of success. Swadeshi is preached as an item of non-co-operation, as a demonstration of the spirit of sacrifice, and it is an item which every man, woman and child can take up.

August 1920.

SPEECH AT BEZWADA

As I said this morning one essential condition for the progress of India is Hindu-Muslim Unity. I understand that there was a little bit of bickering between Hindus and Mussalmans to-day in Bezwada. My brother Maulana Shaukat Ali adjusted the dispute between the two communities and he illustrated in his own person the entire efficacy of one item in the first stage of Non-co-operation. He sat without any vakils appearing before him for either parties to arbitrate on the dispute between them. He required no postponement for the consideration of the question from time to time. His fees consisted in a broken lead pencil. That is what we should do, if all the lawyers suspended practice and set up arbitration for the settlement of private disputes. But why was there any quarrel at all? It is laughable in the extreme when you come to think of it. Because the Hindus seem to have played music whilst passing the mosque. I think it was improper for them to do so. Hindu Moslem Unity does not mean that Hindus should cease to respect the prejudices and sentiments cherished by Mussalmans. And as this question of music has given rise to many a quarrel between the two communities it behoves the Hindus, if they want to cultivate true Hindu-Moslem Unity, to refrain from acts which they know injure the sentiments of their Mussalman brethren. We may not take undue advantage of the great spirit of toleration that is developing in Mussalmans and do things likely to irritate them. It is never a matter of principle for a Hindu procession to continue playing music before mosques. And now that we desire voluntarily to respect Mussalman sentiment, we should be doubly careful at a time when Hindus are offering assistance to Mussalmans in their troubles. That assistance should be given in all humility and without any arrogation of rights. To my Mussalman brethren I would say that it would become their dignity to restrain themselves and not feel irritated when any Hindu had done anything to irritate their religious sentiment. But in any event, you have today presented to you a remedy for the settlement of any such issue. We must settle our disputes by arbitration as was done this afternoon. You cannot always get a Moulana Shankat Ali, exercising unrivalled influence on the community. But we can always get people enough in our own villages, towns and districts who exercise influence over such villages and towns and command the confidence of both the communities. The offended party should consider it its duty to approach them and not to take the law in its own hands.

It gives me much pleasure to announce to you that, Mr. Kaleswar Rao has consented to refrain from standing for election to the new Legislative Councils. You will be also pleased to know that Mr. Gulam Nohiuddin has resigned his Honorary Magistrateship, I hope that both these patriots will not consider that they have done their last duty by their acts of renunciation, but I hope they will regard their acts as a prelude to acts of greater purpose and greater energy and I hope they will take in hand the work of educating the electorate in their districts regarding boycott of councils. I have said elsewhere that never for another century will India be faced with a conjunction of events that faces it to-day. The cloud that has descended upon Islam has solidified the Moslem world as nothing else could have. It has awakened the men and women of Mussulman India from their deep sleep. Inasmuch as a single Panjabi was made to crawl on his belly in the famous street of Amitsar, I hold that the whole of was made to crawl on its belly. And if we want to straighten up ourselves from that crawling position and stand erect before the whole world, it requires, a tremendous effort. H.E. the Viceroy in his Viceregal pronouncement at the opening of the Council was pleased to say that he did not desire to make any remarks on the Punjab events. He treated them as a closed chapter and referred us to the future verdict of history. I venture to tell you the citizens of Bezwada that India will have deserved to crawl in that lane if she accepts this pronouncement as the final answer, and if we want to stand erect before the whole world, it is impossible for a single child, man or woman in India to rest until fullest reparation has been done for the Punjab wrong. Similarly with reference to the Khilafat grievance the Mussalmans of India in my humble opinion will forfeit all title to consider themselves the followers of the great Prophet in whose name they recite the Kalama, day in and day out, they will forfeit their title if they do not put their shoulders to the wheel and lift this cloud that is hanging on them. But we shall make a serious blunder. India will commit suicide, if we do not understand and appreciate the forces that are arrayed against us. We have got to face a mighty Government with all its power ranged against us. This composed of men who are able, courageous, capable of making sacrifices. It is a Government which does not scruple to use means, fair or foul, in order to gain its end. No craft is above that Government. It resorts to frightfulness, terrorism. It resorts to bribery, in the shape of titles, honour and high offices. It administers opiates in the shape of Reforms. In essence then it is an autocracy double distilled in the guise of democracy. The greatest gift of a crafty cunning man are worthless so long as cunning resides in his heart. It is a Government representing a civilisation which is purely material and godless. I have given to you these qualities of this government in order not to excite your angry passions, but in order that you may appreciate the forces that are matched against you. Anger will serve no purpose. We shall have to meet ungodliness by godliness. We shall have to meet their untruth by truth; we shall have to meet their cunning and their craft by openness and simplicity; we shall have to meet their terrorism and frightfulness by bravery. And it is an unbending bravery which is demanded of every man, woman and child. We must meet their organisation by greater organising ability. We must meet their discipline by grater discipline, and we must meet their sacrifices by infinitely greater sacrifices, and if we are in a position to show these qualities in a full measure I have not the slightest doubt that we shall win this battle. If really we have fear of God in us, our prayers will give us the strength to secure victory. God has always come to the help of the helpless and we need not go before any earthly power for help.

You heard this morning of the bravery of the sword, and the bravery of suffering. For me personally I have forever rejected the bravery of the sword. But, to-day it is not my purpose to demonstrate to you the final ineffectiveness of the sword. But he who runs may see that before India possesses itself a sword which will be more than a match for the forces of Europe, it will he generations. India may resort to the destruction of life and property here and there but such destructive cases serve no purpose. I have therefore presented to you a weapon called the bravery of suffering, otherwise called Non-co-operation. It is a bravery which is open to the weakest among the weak. It is open to women and children. The power of suffering is the prerogative of nobody, and if only 300 millions of Indians could show the power of suffering in order to redress a grievous wrong done to the nation or to its religion, I make bold to say that, India will never require to draw the sword. And unless we are able to show an adequate measure of sacrifice we shall lose this battle. No one need tell me that India has not got this power of suffering. Every father and mother is witness to what i am about to say, viz., that every father and mother have shown in the domestic affairs matchless power of suffering. And if we have only developed national consciousness, if we have developed sufficient regard for our religion, we shall have developed power of suffering in the national and religious field. Considered in these terms the first stage in Non-co-operation is the simplest and the easiest state. If the title-holders of India consider that India is suffering from a grievous wrong both as regards the Punjab and the Khilafat is it any suffering on their part to renounce their titles to-day? What is the measure of the suffering awaiting the lawyers who are called upon to suspend practice when compared to the great benefit which is in store for the nation? And if thy parents of India will summon up courage to sacrifice secular education, they will have given their children the real education of a life-time. For they will have learnt the value of religion and national honour. And I ask you, the citizens of Bezwada, to think well before you accept the loaves and fishes in the form of Government offices set them on one side and set national honour on the other and make your service. What sacrifice is there involved in the individual renouncing his candidature for legislative councils. The councils are a tempting bait. All kinds of arguments are being advanced in favour of joining the councils. India will sacrifice the opportunity of gaining her liberty if she touches them. It passes comprehension how we, who have known this Government, who have read the Viceregal pronouncement, how we who have known their determination not to give justice in the Punjab and the Khilafat matters, can gain any benefit by co-operation, constructive or obstructive, with this Government? But the Nationalists, belonging to a great popular party, tell us that if they do not contest these scats, the moderates will get in. Surely, it is nothing but an exhibition of want of courage and faith in our own cause to feel that we must enter the councils lest moderates should get in. Moderates believe in the possibility of obtaining justice at the hands of the Government. Nationalists have on the other hand filled the platforms with denunciations of the Government and its measures. How can the Nationalists ever hope to gain anything by entering the councils, holding the belief that they do? They will better represent the popular will if they wring justice from the Government by means of Non-co-operation. A calculating spirit at the present moment in the history of India will prove its ruin. I, therefore, tender my hearty congratulation to those who have announced their resignations of candidature or honorary offices, and I hope that their example will prove infectious. I have been told, and I believe it myself from what I have seen, that the Andhrus are a brave, courageous and spiritually-inclined people. I venture therefore to ask my Andhra brethren whether they have understood the spirituality of this beautiful doctrine of Non-co-operation. If they have, I hope they will not wait for a single moment for a mandate from the Congress or the Moslem League. They will understand that a spiritual weapon is god whether it is wielded by one or many. I, therefore, invite you to go to Calcutta with a united will and a united purpose, sanctified by a spirit of sacrifice, with a will of your own to convert those who are still undecided about the spirituality or the practicability of the weapon.

I thank you for the attention and patience with which you have listened to me. I pray to the Almighty that He may give you wisdom and courage that are so necessary at the present moment.--

August 1920.

THE CONGRESS

The largest and the most important Congress ever held has come and gone, It was the biggest demonstration ever held against the present system of Government. The President uttered the whole truth when he said that it was a Congress in which, instead of the President and the leaders driving the people, the people drove him and the latter. It was clear to every one on the platform that the people had taken the reins in their own hands. The platform would gladly have moved at a slower pace.

The Congress gave one day to a full discussion of the creed and voted solidly for it with but two dissentients after two nights' sleep over the discussion. It gave one day to a discussion of non-co-operation resolution and voted for it with unparalleled enthusiasm. It gave the last day to listening to the whole of the remaining thirty-two Articles of the Constitution which were read and translated word for word by Maulana Mahomed Ali in a loud and clear voice. It showed that it was intelligently following the reading of it, for there was dissent when Article Eight was reached. It referred to non-interference by the Congress in the internal affairs of the Native States. The Congress would not have passed the proviso if it had meant that it could even voice the feelings of the people residing in the territories ruled by the princes. Happily it resolution suggesting the advisability of establishing Responsible Government in their territories enabled me to illustrate to the audience that the proviso did not preclude the Congress from ventilating the grievances and aspirations of the subjects of these states, whilst it clearly prevented the Congress from taking any executive action in connection with them; as for instance holding a hostile demonstration in the Native States against any action of theirs. The Congress claims to dictate to the Government but it cannot do so by the very nature of its constitution in respect of the Native States.

Thus the Congress has taken three important steps after the greatest deliberation. It has expressed its determination in the clearest possible terms to attain complete null-government, if possible still in association with the British people, but even without, if necessary. It proposes to do so only by means that are honourable and non-violent. It has introduced fundamental changes in the constitution regulating its activities and has performed an act of self-denial in voluntarily restricting the number of delegates to one for every fifty thousand of the population of India and has insisted upon the delegates being the real representatives of those who want to take any part in the political life of the country. And with a view to ensuring the representation of all political parties it has accepted the principle of "single transferable vote." It has reaffirmed the non-co-operation resolution of the Special Session and amplified it in every respect. It has emphasised the necessity of non-violence and laid down that the attainment of Swaraj is conditional upon the complete harmony between the component parts of India, and has therefore inculcated Hindu-Muslim unity. The Hindu delegates have called upon their leaders to settle disputes between Brahmins and non-Brahmins and have urged upon the religious heads the necessity of getting rid of the poison of untouchability. The Congress has told the parents of school-going children, and the lawyers that they have not responded sufficiently to the call of the nation and that they must make greater effort in doing so. It therefore follows that the lawyers who do not respond quickly to the call for suspension and the parents who persist in keeping their children in Government and aided institutions must find themselves dropping out from the public life of the country. The country calls upon every man and woman in India to do their full share. But of the details of the non-co-operation resolution I must write later.

WHO IS DISLOYAL?

Mr. Montagu has discovered a new definition of disloyalty. He considers my suggestion to boycott the visit of the Prince of Wales to be disloyal and some newspapers taking the cue from him have called persons who have made the suggestion 'unmannerly'. They have even attributed to these 'unmannerly' persons the suggestion of boycotting the Prince. I draw a sharp and fundamental distinction between boycotting the Prince and boycotting any welcome arranged for him. Personally I would extend the heartiest welcome to His Royal Highness if he came or could come without official patronage and the protecting wings of the Government of the day. Being the heir to a constitutional monarch, the Prince's movements are regulated and dictated by the ministers, no matter how much the dictation may be concealed beneath diplomatically polite language. In suggesting the boycott therefore the promoters have suggested boycott of an insolent bureaucracy and dishonest ministers of his Majesty.

You cannot have it both ways. It is true that under a constitutional monarchy, the royalty is above politics. But you cannot send the Prince on a political visit for the purpose of making political capital out of him, and then complain that those who will not play your game and in order to checkmate you, proclaim boycott of the Royal visit do not know constitutional usage. For the Prince's visit is not for pleasure. His Royal Highness is to come in Mr.

Lloyd George's words, as the "ambassador of the British nation," in other words, his own ambassador in order to issue a certificate of merit to him and possibly to give the ministers a new lease of life. The wish is designed to consolidate and strengthen a power that spells mischief for India. Even us it is, Mr. Montagu has foreseen, that the welcome will probably be excelled by any hitherto extended to Royalty, meaning that the people are not really and deeply affected and stirred by the official atrocities in the Punjab and the manifestly dishonest breach of official declarations on the Khilafat. With the knowledge that India was bleeding at heart, the Government of India should have told His Majesty's ministers that the moment was inopportune for sending the Prince. I venture to submit that it is adding insult to injury to bring the Prince and through his visit to steal honours and further prestige for a Government that deserves to be dismissed with disgrace. I claim that I prove my loyalty by saying that India is in no mood, is too deeply in mourning, to take part in and to welcome His Royal Highness, and that the ministers and the Indian Government show their disloyalty by making the Prince a catspaw of their deep political game. If they persist, it is the clear duty of India to have nothing to do with the visit.

CRUSADE AGAINST NON-CO-OPERATION

I have most carefully read the manifesto addressed by Sir Narayan Chandavarkar and others dissuading the people from joining the non co-operation movement. I had expected to find some solid argument against non-co-operation, but to my great regret I have found in it nothing but distortion (no doubt unconscious) of the great religions and history. The manifesto says that 'non-co-operation is deprecated by the religious tenets and traditions of our motherland, nay, of all the religions that have saved and elevated the human race.' I venture to submit that the Bhagwad Gita is a gospel of non-co-operation between forces of darkness and those of light. If it is to be literally interpreted Arjun representing a just cause was enjoined to engage in bloody warfare with the unjust Kauravas. Tulsidas advises the Sant (the good) to shun the Asant (the evil-doers). The Zendavesta represents a perpetual dual between Ormuzd and Ahriman, between whom there is no compromise. To say of the Bible that it taboos non-co-operation is not to know Jesus, a Prince among passive resisters, who uncompromisingly challenged the might of the Sadducees and the Pharisees and for the sake of truth did not hesitate to divide sons from their parents. And what did the Prophet of Islam do? He non-co-operated in Mecca in a most active manner so long as his life was not in danger and wiped the dust of Mecca off his feet when he found that he and his followers might have uselessly to perish, and fled to Medina and returned when he was strong enough to give battle to his opponents. The duty of non-co-operation with unjust men and kings is as strictly enjoined by all the religions as is the duty of co-operation with just men and kings. Indeed most of the scriptures of the world seem even to go beyond non-co-operation and prefer a violence to effeminate submission to a wrong. The Hindu religious tradition of which the manifesto speaks, clearly proves the duty of non-co-operation. Prahlad dissociated himself from his father, Meerabai from her husband, Bibhishan from his brutal brother.

The manifesto speaking of the secular aspect says, 'The history of nations affords no instance to show that it (meaning non-co-operation) has, when employed, succeeded and done good,' One most recent instance of brilliant success of non-co-operation is that of General Botha who boycotted Lord Milner's reformed councils and thereby procured a perfect constitution for his country. The Dukhobours of Russia offered non-co-operation, and a handful though they were, their grievances so deeply moved the civilized world that Canada offered them a home where they form a prosperous community. In India instances can be given by the dozen, in which in little principalities the raiyats when deeply grieved by their chiefs have cut off all connection with them and bent them to their will. I know of no instance in history where well-managed non-co-operation has failed.

Hitherto I have given historical instances of bloodless non-co-operation, I will not insult the intelligence of the reader by citing historical instances of non-co-operation combined with, violence, but I am free to confess that there are on record as many successes as failures in violent non-co-operation. And it is because I know this fact that I have placed before the country a non-violent scheme in which, if at all worked satisfactorily, success is a certainty and in which non-response means no harm. For if even one man non-co-operates, say, by resigning some office, he has gained, not lost. That is its ethical or religious aspect. For its political result naturally it requires polymerous support. I fear therefore no disastrous result from non-co-operation save for an outbreak of violence on the part of the people whether under provocation or otherwise. I would risk violence a thousand times than risk the emasculation of a whole race.

SPEECH AT MUZAFFARABAD

Before a crowded meeting of Mussalmans in the Muzaffarabad, Bombay, held on the 29th July 1920, speaking on the impending non-co-operation which commenced on the 1st of August, Mr. Gandhi said: The time for speeches on non-co-operation was past and the time for practice had arrived. But two things were needful for complete success. An environment free from any violence on the part of the people and a spirit of self-sacrifice. Non-co-operation, as the speaker had conceived it, was an impossibility in an atmosphere surcharged with the spirit of violence. Violence was an exhibition of anger and any such exhibition was dissipation of valuable energy. Subduing of one's anger was a storing up of national energy, which, when set free in an ordered manner, would produce astounding results. His conception of non-co-operation did not involve rapine, plunder, incendiarism and all the concomitants of mass madness. His scheme presupposed ability on their part to control all the forces of evil. If, therefore, any disorderliness was found on the part of the people which they could not control, he for one would certainly help the Government to control them. In the presence of disorder it would be for him a choice of evil, and evil through he considered the present Government to be, he would not hesitate for the time being to help the Government to control disorder. But he had faith in the people. He believed that they knew that the cause could only be won by non-violent methods. To put it at the lowest, the people had not the power, even if they had the will, to resist with brute strength the unjust Governments of Europe who had, in the intoxication of their success disregarding every canon of justice dealt so cruelly by the only Islamic Power in Europe.

In non-co-operation they had a matchless and powerful weapon. It was a sign of religious atrophy to sustain an unjust Government that supported an injustice by resorting to untruth and camouflage. So long therefore as the Government did not purge itself of the canker of injustice and untruth, it was their duty to withdraw all help from it consistently with their ability to preserve order in the social structure. The first stage of non-co-operation was therefore arranged so as to involve minimum of danger to public peace and minimum of sacrifice on the part of those who participated in the movement. And if they might not help an evil Government nor receive any favours from it, it followed that they must give up all titles of honour which were no longer a proud possession. Lawyers, who were in reality honorary officers of the Court, should cease to support Courts that uphold the prestige of an unjust Government and the people must be able to settle their disputes and quarrels by private arbitration. Similarly parents should withdraw their children from the public schools and they must evolve a system of national education or private education totally independent of the Government. An insolent Government conscious of its brute strength, might laugh at such withdrawals by the people especially as the Law courts and schools were supposed to help the people, but he had not a shadow of doubt that the moral effect of such a step could not possibly be lost even upon a Government whose conscience had become stifled by the intoxication of power.

He had hesitation in accepting Swadeshi as a plank in non-co-operation. To him Swadeshi was as dear as life itself. But he had no desire to smuggle in Swadeshi through the Khilafat movement, if it could not legitimately help that movement, but conceived as non-co-operation was, in a spirit of self-sacrifice, Swadeshi had a legitimate place in the movement. Pure Swadeshi meant sacrifice of the liking for fineries. He asked the nation to sacrifice its liking for the fineries of Europe and Japan and be satisfied with the coarse but beautiful fabrics woven on their handlooms out of yarns spun by millions of their sisters. If the nation had become really awakened to a sense of the danger to its religions and its self-respect, it could not but perceive the absolute and immediate necessity of the adoption of Swadeshi in its intense form and if the people of India adopted Swadeshi with the religious zeal he begged to assure them that its adoption would arm them with a new power and would produce an unmistakable impression throughout the whole world. He, therefore, expected the Mussalmans to give the lead by giving up all the fineries they were so fond of and adopt the simple cloth that could be produced by the manual labour of their sisters and brethren in their own cottages. And he hoped that the Hindus would follow suit. It was a sacrifice in which the whole nation, every man, woman and child could take part.

RIDICULE REPLACING REPRESSION

Had His Excellency the Viceroy not made it impossible by his defiant attitude on the Punjab and the Khilafat, I would have tendered him hearty congratulations for substituting ridicule for repression in order to kill a movement distasteful to him. For, torn from its context and read by itself His Excellency's discourse on non-co-operation is unexceptionable. It is a symptom of translation from savagery to civilization. Pouring ridicule on one's opponent is an approved method in civilised politics. And if the method is consistently continued, it will mark an important improvement upon the official barbarity of the Punjab. His interpretation of Mr. Montagu's statement about the movement is also not open to any objection whatsoever. Without doubt a government has the right to use sufficient force to put down an actual outbreak of violence.

But I regret to have to confess that this attempt to pour ridicule on the movement, read in conjunction with the sentiments on the Punjab and the Khilafat, preceding the ridicule, seems to show that His Excellency has made it a virtue of necessity. He has not finally abandoned the method of terrorism and frightfulness, but he finds the movement being conducted in such an open and truthful manner that any attempt to kill it by violent repression would not expose him not only to ridicule but contempt of all right-thinking men.

Let us however examine the adjectives used by His Excellency to kill the movement by laughing at it. It is 'futile,' 'ill-advised,' 'intrinsically insane,' 'unpractical,' 'visionary.' He has rounded off the adjectives by describing the movement as 'most foolish of all foolish schemes.' His Excellency has become so impatient of it that he has used all his vocabulary for showing the magnitude of the ridiculous nature of non-co-operation.

Unfortunately for His Excellency the movement is likely to grow with ridicule as it is certain to flourish on repression. No vital movement can be killed except by the impatience, ignorance or laziness of its authors. A movement cannot be 'insane' that is conducted by men of action as I claim the members of the Non-co-operation Committee are. It is hardly 'unpractical,' seeing that if the people respond, every one admits that it will achieve the end. At the same time it is perfectly true that if there is no response from the people, the movement will be popularly described as 'visionary.' It is for the nation to return an effective answer by organised non-co-operation and change ridicule into respect. Ridicule is like repression. Both give place to respect when they fail to produce the intended effect.

THE VICEREGAL PRONOUNCEMENT

It may be that having lost faith in His Excellency's probity and capacity to hold the high office of Viceroy of India, I now read his speeches with a biased mind, but the speech His Excellency delivered at the time of opening of the council shows to me a mental attitude which makes association with him or his Government impossible for self-respecting men.

The remarks on the Punjab mean a flat refusal to grant redress. He would have us to 'concentrate on the problems of the immediate future!' The immediate future is to compel repentance on the part of the Government on the Punjab matter. Of this there is no sign. On the contrary, His Excellency resists the temptation to reply to his critics, meaning thereby that he has not changed his opinion on the many vital matters affecting the honour of India. He is 'content to leave the issues to the verdict of history.' Now this kind of language, in my opinion, is calculated further to inflame the Indian mind. Of what use can a favourable verdict of history be to men who have been wronged and who are still under the heels of officers who have shown themselves utterly unfit to hold offices of trust and responsibility? The plea for co-operation is, to say the least, hypocritical in the face of the determination to refuse justice to the Punjab. Can a patient who is suffering from an intolerable ache be soothed by the most tempting dishes placed before him? Will he not consider it mockery on the part of the physician who so tempted him without curing him of his pain?

His Excellency is, if possible, even less happy on the Khilafat. "So far as any Government could," says this trustee for the nation, "we pressed upon the Peace Conference the views of Indian Moslems. But notwithstanding our efforts on their behalf we are threatened with a campaign of non-co-operation because, forsooth, the allied Powers found themselves unable to accept the contentions advanced by Indian Moslems." This is most misleading if not untruthful. His Excellency knows that the peace terms are not the work of the allied Powers. He knows that Mr. Lloyd George is the prime author of terms and that the latter has never repudiated his responsibility for them. He has with amazing audacity justified them in spite of his considered pledge to the Moslems of India regarding Constantinople, Thrace and the rich and renowned lands of Asia minor. It is not truthful to saddle responsibility for the terms on the allied Powers when Great Britain alone has promoted them. The offence of the Viceroy becomes greater when we remember that he admits the justness of the Muslim claim. He could not have 'pressed' it if he did not admit its justice.

I venture to think that His Excellency by his pronouncement on the Punjab has strengthened the nation in its efforts to seek a remedy to compel redress of the two wrongs before it can make anything of the so-called Reforms.

FROM RIDICULE, TO--?

It will be admitted that non-co-operation has passed the stage ridicule. Whether it will now be met by repression or respect remains to be seen. Opinion has already been expressed in these columns that ridicule is an approved and civilized method of opposition. The viceregal ridicule though expressed in unnecessarily impolite terms was not open to exception.

But the testing time has now arrived. In a civilized country when ridicule fails to kill a movement it begins to command respect. Opponents meet it by respectful and cogent argument and the mutual behaviour of rival parties never becomes violent. Each party seeks to convert the other or draw the uncertain element towards its side by pure argument and reasoning.

There is little doubt now that the boycott of the councils will be extensive if it is not complete. The students have become disturbed. Important institutions may any day become truly national. Pandit Motilal Nehru's great renunciation of a legal practice which was probably second to nobody's is by itself an event calculated to change ridicule into respect. It ought to set people thinking seriously about their own attitude. There must be something very wrong about our Government--to warrant the step

Pundit Motilal Nehru has taken. Post graduate students have given up their fellowships. Medical students have refused to appear for their final examination. Non-co-operation in these circumstances cannot be called an inane movement.

Either the Government must bend to the will of the people which is being expressed in no unmistakable terms through non-co-operation, or it must attempt to crush the movement by repression.

Any force used by a government under any circumstance is not repression. An open trial of a person accused of having advocated methods of violence is not repression. Every State has the right to put down or prevent violence by force. But the trial of Mr. Zafar Ali Khan and two Moulvis of Panipat shows that the Government is seeking not to put down or prevent violence but to suppress expression of opinion, to prevent the spread of disaffection. This is repression. The trials are the beginning of it. It has not still assumed a virulent form but if these trials do not result in stilling the propaganda, it is highly likely that severe repression will be resorted to by the Government.

The only other way to prevent the spread of disaffection is to remove the causes thereof. And that would be to respect the growing response of the country to the programme of non-co-operation. It is too much to expect repentance and humility from a government intoxicated with success and power.

We must therefore assume that the second stage in the Government programme will be repression growing in violence in the same ratio as the progress of non-co-operation. And if the movement survives repression, the day of victory of truth is near. We must then be prepared for prosecutions, punishments even up to deportations. We must evolve the capacity for going on with our programme without the leaders. That means capacity for self-government. And as no government in the world can possibly put a whole nation in prison, it must yield to its demand or abdication in favour of a government suited to that nation.

It is clear that abstention from violence and persistence in the programme are our only and surest chance of attaining our end.

The government has its choice, either to respect the movement or to try to repress it by barbarous methods. Our choice is either to succumb to repression or to continue in spite of repression.

TO EVERY ENGLISHMAN IN INDIA

Dear Friend,

I wish that every Englishman will see this appeal and give thoughtful attention to it.

Let me introduce myself to you. In my humble opinion no Indian has co-operated with the British Government more than I have for an unbroken period of twenty-nine years of public life in the face of circumstances that might well have turned any other man into a rebel. I ask you to believe me when I tell you that my co-operation was not based on the fear of the punishments provided by your laws or any other selfish motives. It was free and voluntary co-operation based on the belief that the sum total of the activity of the British Government was for the benefit of India. I put my life in peril four times for the sake of the Empire,--at the time of the Boer war when I was in charge of the Ambulance corps whose work was mentioned in General Buller's dispatches, at the time of the Zulu revolt in Natal when I was in charge of a similar corps at the time of the commencement of the late war when I raised an Ambulance corps and as a result of the strenuous training had a severe attack of pleurisy, and lastly, in fulfilment of my promise to Lord Chelmsford at the War Conference in Delhi. I threw myself in such an active recruiting campaign in Kuira District involving long and trying marches that I had an attack of dysentry which proved almost fatal. I did all this in the full belief that acts such as mine must gain for my country an equal status in the Empire. So late as last December I pleaded hard for a trustful co-operation, I fully believed that Mr. Lloyd George would redeem his promise to the Mussalmans and that the revelations of the official atrocities in the Punjab would secure full reparation for the Punjabis. But the treachery of Mr. Lloyd George and its appreciation by you, and the condonation of the Punjab atrocities have completely shattered my faith in the good intentions of the Government and the nation which is supporting it.

But though, my faith in your good intentions is gone, I recognise your bravery and I know that what you will not yield to justice and reason, you will gladly yield to bravery.

See what this Empire means to India

Exploitation of India's resources for the benefit of Great Britain.

An ever-increasing military expenditure, and a civil service the most expensive in the world.

Extravagant working of every department in utter disregard of India's poverty.

Disarmament and consequent emasculation of a whole nation lest an armed nation might imperil the lives of a handful of you in our midst. Traffic in intoxicating liquors and drugs for the purposes of sustaining a top heavy administration.

Progressively representative legislation in order to suppress an evergrowing agitation seeking to give expression to a nation's agony.

Degrading treatment of Indians residing in your dominions, and

You have shown total disregard of our feelings by glorifying the Punjab administration and flouting the Mosulman sentiment.

I know you would not mind if we could fight and wrest the sceptre form your hands. You know that we are powerless to do that, for you have ensured our incapacity to fight in open and honourable battle. Bravery on the battlefield is thus impossible for us. Bravery of the soul still remains open to us. I know you will respond to that also. I am engaged in evoking that bravery. Non-co-operation means nothing less than training in self-sacrifice. Why should we co-operate with you when we know that by your administration of this great country we are lifting daily enslaved in an increasing degree. This response of the people to my appeal is not due to my personality. I would like you to dismiss me, and for that matter the Ali Brothers too, from your consideration. My personality will fail to evoke any response to anti-Muslim cry if I were foolish enough to rise it, as the magic name of the Ali Brothers would fail to inspire the Mussalmans with enthusiasm if they were madly to raise in anti-Hindu cry. People flock in their thousands to listen to us because we to-day represent the voice of a nation groaning under iron heels. The Ali Brothers were your friends as I was, and still am. My religion forbids me to bear any ill-will towards you. I would not raise my hand against you even if I had the power. I expect to conquer you only by my suffering. The Ali Brothers will certainly draw the sword, if they could, in defence of their religion and their country. But they and I have made common cause with the people of India in their attempt to voice their feelings and to find a remedy for their distress.

You are in search of a remedy to suppress this rising ebullition of national feeling. I venture to suggest to you that the only way to suppress it is to remove the causes. You have yet the power. You can repent of the wrongs done to Indians. You can compel Mr. Lloyd George to redeem his promises. I assure you he has kept many escape doors. You can compel the Viceroy to retire in favour of a better one, you can revise your ideas about Sir Michael O'Dwyer and General Dyer. You can compel the Government to summon a conference of the recognised lenders of the people, duly elected by them and representing all shades of opinion so as to devise means for granting *Swaraj* in accordance with the wishes of the people of India. But this you cannot do unless you consider every Indian to be in reality your equal and brother. I ask for no patronage, I merely point out to you, as a friend, as honourable solution of a grave problem. The other solution, namely repression is open to YOU. I prophesy that it will fail. It has begun already. The Government has already imprisoned two brave men of Panipat for holding and expressing their opinions freely. Another is on his trial in Lahore for having expressed similar opinion. One in the Oudh District is already imprisoned. Another awaits judgment. You should know what is going on in your midst. Our propaganda is being carried on in anticipation of repression. I invite you respectfully to choose the better way and make common cause with the people of India whose salt you are eating. To seek to thwart their inspirations is disloyalty to the country.

I am, Your faithful friend, M. K. GANDHI

ONE STEP ENOUGH FOR ME

Mr. Stokes is a Christian, who wants to follow the light that God gives him. He has adopted India as his home. He is watching the non-co-operation movement from the Kotgarh hills where he is living in isolation from the India of the plains and serving the hillmen. He has contributed three articles on non-co-operation to the columns of the Servant of Calcutta and other papers. I had the pleasure of reading them during my Bengal tour. Mr. Stokes approves of non-co-operation but dreads the consequences that may follow complete success

i.e.,

evacuation of India by the British. He conjures up before his mind a picture of India invaded by the Afghans from the North-West, plundered by the Gurkhas from the Hills. For me I say with Cardinal Newman: 'I do not ask to see the distant scene; one step enough for me.' The movement is essentially religious. The business of every god-fearing man is to dissociate himself from evil in total disregard of consequences. He must have faith in a good deed producing only a good result: that in my opinion is the Gita doctrine of work without attachment. God does not permit him to peep into the future. He follows truth although the following of it may endanger his very life. He knows that it is better to die in the way of God than to live in the way of Satan. Therefore who ever is satisfied that this Government represents the activity of Satan has no choice left to him but to dissociate himself from it.

However, let us consider the worst that can happen to India on a sudden evacuation of India by the British. What does it matter that the Gurkhas and the Pathans attack us? Surely we would be better able to deal with their violence than we are with the continued violence, moral and physical, perpetrated by the present Government. Mr. Stokes does not seem to eschew the use of physical force. Surely the combined labour of the Rajput, the Sikh and the Mussalman warriors in a united India may be trusted to deal with plunderers from any or all the sides. Imagine however the worst: Japan overwhelming us from the Bay of Bengal, the Gurkhas from the Hills, and the Pathans from the North-West. If we not succeed in driving them out we make terms with them and drive them at the first opportunity. This will be a more manly course than a hopeless submission to an admittedly wrongful State.

But I refuse to contemplate the dismal out-look. If the movement succeeds through non-violent non-co-operation, and that is the supposition Mr. Stokes has started with, the English whether they remain or retire, they will do so as friends and under a well-ordered agreement as between partners. I still believe in the goodness of human nature, whether it is English or any other. I therefore do not believe that the English will leave in a night.

And do I consider the Gurkha and the Afghan being incorrigible thieves and robbers without ability to respond to purifying influences? I do not. If India returns to her spirituality, it will react upon the neighbouring tribes, she will interest herself in the welfare of these hardy but poor people, and even support them if necessary, not out of fear but as a matter of neighbourly duty. She will have dealt with Japan simultaneously with the British. Japan will not want to invade India, if India has learnt to consider it a sin to use a single foreign article that she can manufacture within her own borders. She produces enough to eat and her men and women can without difficulty manufacture enough to clothe to cover their nakedness and protect themselves from heat and cold. We become prey to invasion if we excite the greed of foreign nation, by dealing with them under a feeling dependence on them. We must learn to be independent of every one of them.

Whether therefore we finally succeed through violence or non-violence in my opinion, the prospect is by no means so gloomy as Mr. Stokes has imagined. Any conceivable prospect is, in my opinion, less black than the present unmanly and helpless condition. And we cannot do better than following out fearlessly and with confidence the open and honourable programme of non-violence and sacrifice that we have mapped for ourselves.

THE NEED FOR HUMILITY

The spirit of non-violence necessarily leads to humility. Non-violence means reliance on God, the Rocks of ages. If we would seek His aid, we must approach Him with a humble and a contrite heart. Non-co-operationists may not trade upon their amazing success at the Congress. We must act, even as the mango tree which drops as it bears fruit. Its grandeur lies in its majestic lowliness. But one hears of non-co-operationists being insolent and intolerant in their behaviour towards those who differ from them. I know that they will lose all their majesty and glory, if they betray any inflation. Whilst we may not be dissatisfied with the progress made so far, we have little to our credit to make us feel proud. We have to sacrifice much more than we have done to justify pride, much less elation. Thousands, who flocked to the Congress pandal, have undoubtedly given their intellectual assent to the doctrine but few have followed it out in practice. Leaving aside the pleaders, how many parents have withdrawn their children from schools? How many of those who registered their vote in favour of non-co-operation have taken to hand-spinning or discarded the use of all foreign cloth?

Non-co-operation is not a movement of brag, bluster, or bluff. It is a test of our sincerity. It requires solid and silent self-sacrifice. It challenges our honesty and our capacity for national work. It is a movement that aims at translating ideas into action. And the more we do, the more we find that much more must be done than we have expected. And this thought of our imperfection must make us humble.

A non-co-operationist strives to compel attention and to set an example not by his violence but by his unobtrusive humility. He allows his solid action to speak for his creed. His strength lies in his reliance upon the correctness of his position. And the conviction of it grows most in his opponent when he least interposes his speech between his action and his opponent. Speech, especially when it is haughty, betrays want of confidence and it makes one's opponent sceptical about the reality of the act itself. Humility therefore is the key to quick success. I hope that every non-co-operationist will recognise the necessity of being humble and self-restrained. It is because so little is really required to be done because all of that little depends entirely upon ourselves that I have ventured the belief that Swaraj is attainable in less than one year.

SOME QUESTIONS ANSWERED

"I write to thank you for yours of the 7th instant and especially for your request that I should after reading your writings in "Young India" on non-co-operation, give a full and frank criticism of them. I know that your sole desire is to find out the truth and to act accordingly, and hence I venture to make the following remarks. In the issue of May 5th you say that non-co-operation is "not even anti-Government." But surely to refuse to have anything to do with the Government to the extent of not serving it and of not paying its taxes is actually, if not theoretically anti-Government; and such a course must ultimately make all Government impossible. Again, you say, "It is the inherent right of a subject to refuse to assist a government that will not listen to him." Leaving aside the question of the ethical soundness of this proposition, may I ask which Government, in the present case? Has not the Indian Government done all it possibly can in the matter? Then if its attempts to voice the request of India should fail, would it be fair and just to do anything against it? Would not the proper course be non-co-operation with the Supreme Council of the Allies, including Great Britain, if it be found that the latter has failed properly to support the demand of the Indian Government and people? It seems to me that in all your writings and speeches you forget that in the present question both Government and people are as one, and if they fail to get what they justly want, how does the question of non-co-operation arise? Hindus and Englishmen and the Government are all at present "shouldering in a full-hearted manner the burden that Muhomedans of India are carrying etc. etc." But supposing we fail of our object--what then? Are we all to refuse to co-operate and with whom?

Might I recommend the consideration of the following course of conduct?

(1) "Wait and see" what the actual terms of the Treaty with Turkey are?

(2) If they are not in accordance with the aspirations and recommendations of the Government and the people of India, the every legitimate effort should be made to have the terms revised.

(3) To the bitter end, co-operate with a Government that co-operates with us, and only when it refuses co-operation, go in for non-co-operation.

So far I personally see no reason whatsoever for non-co-operation with the Indian Government, and till it fails to voice the needs and demands of India as a whole there can be no reason. The Indian Government does some times make mistakes, but in the Khilafat matter it is sound and therefore deserves or ought to have the sympathetic and whole-hearted co-operation of every one in India. I hope that you will kindly consider the above and perhaps you will be able to find time for a reply in *Young India*."

I gladly make room for the above letter and respond to the suggestion to give a public reply as no doubt the difficulty experienced by the English friend is experienced by many. Causes are generally lost, not owing to the determined opposition of men who will not see the truth as they want to perpetuate an injustice but because they are able to enlist in their favour the allegiance of those who are anxious to understand a particular cause and take sides after mature judgment. It is only by patient argument with such honest men that one is able to check oneself, correct one's own errors of judgment and at times to wean them from their error and bring them over to one's side. This Khilafat question is specially difficult because there are so many side-issues. It is therefore no wonder that many have more or less difficulty in making up their minds. It is further complicated because the painful necessity for some direct action has arisen in connection with it. But whatever the difficulty, I am convinced that there is no question so important as this one if we want harmony and peace in India.

My friend objects to my statement that non-co-operation is not anti-Government, because he considers that refusal to serve it and pay its taxes is actually anti-Government. I respectfully dissent from the view. If a brother has fundamental differences with his brother, and association with the latter involves his partaking of what in his opinion is an injustice. I hold that it is brotherly duty to refrain from serving his brother and sharing his earnings with him. This happens in everyday life. Prahalad did not act against his father, when he declined to associate himself with the latter's blasphemies. Nor was Jesus anti-Jewish when he declaimed against the Pharisees and the hypocrites, and would have none of them. In such matters, is it not intention that determines the character of a particular act? It is hardly correct as the friend suggests that withdrawal of association under general circumstances would make all government impossible. But it is true that such withdrawal would make all injustice impossible.

My correspondent considers that the Government of India having done all it possibly could, non-co-operation could not be applicable to that Government. In my opinion, whilst it is true that the Government of India has done a great deal, it has not done half as much as it might have done, and might even now do. No Government can absolve itself from further action beyond protesting, when it realises that the people whom it represents feel as keenly as do lakhs of Indian Mussalmans in the Khilafat question. No amount of sympathy with a starving man can possibly avail. He must have bread or he dies, and what is wanted at that critical moment is some exertion to fetch the wherewithal to feed the dying man. The Government of India can to-day heed the agitation and ask, to the point of insistence for full vindication of the pledged word of a British Minister. Has the Government of India resigned by way of protest against the threatened, shameful betrayal of trust on the part of Mr. Lloyd George? Why does the Government of India hide itself behind secret despatches? At a less critical moment Lord Hardiage committed a constitutional indiscretion, openly sympathised with

South African Passive Resistance movement and stemmed the surging tide of public indignation in India, though at the same time he incurred the wrath of the then South African Cabinet and some public men in Great Britain. After all, the utmost that the Government of India has done is on its own showing to transmit and press the Mahomedan claim. Was that not the least it could have done? Could it have done anything less without covering itself with disgrace? What Indian Mahomedans and the Indian public expect the Government of India to do at this critical juncture is not the least, but the utmost that it could do. Viceroys have been known to tender resignations for much smaller causes. Wounded pride brought forth not very long ago the resignation of a Lieutenant Governor. On the Khilafat question, a sacred cause dear to the hearts of several million Mahomedans is in danger of being wounded. I would therefore invite the English friend, and every Englishman in India, and every Hindu, be he moderate or extremist, to make common cause with the Mahomedans and thereby compel the Government of India to do its duty, and thereby compel His Majesty's Ministers to do theirs.

There has been much talk of violence ensuing from active non-co-operation. I venture to suggest that the Mussalmans of India, if they had nothing in the shape of non-co-operation in view, would have long ago yielded to counsels of despair. I admit that non-co-operation is not unattended with danger. But violence is a certainty without, violence is only a possibility with non-co-operation. And it will he a greater possibility if all the important men, English, Hindu and others of the country discountenance it.

I think, that the recommendation made by the friend is being literally followed by the Mahomedans. Although they practically know the fate, they are waiting for the actual terms of the treaty with Turkey. They are certainly going to try every means at their disposal to have the terms revised before beginning non-co-operation. And there will certainly be no non-co-operation commenced so long as there is even hope of active co-operation on the part of the Government of India with the Mahomedans, that is, co-operation strong enough to secure a revision of the terms should they be found to be in conflict with the pledges of British statesmen. But if all these things fail, can Mahomedans as men of honour who hold their religion dearer than their lives do anything less than wash their hands clean of the guilt of British Ministers and the Government of India by refusing to co-operate with them? And can Hindus and Englishmen, if they value Mahomedan friendship, and if they admit then full justice of the Mahomaden friendship and if they admit the full justice of the Mahomedan claim do otherwise than heartily support the Mahomedans by word and deed.

PLEDGES BROKEN

After the forgoing was printed the long-expected peace terms regarding Turkey were received. In my humble opinion they are humiliating to the Supreme Council, to the British ministers, and if as a Hindu with deep reverence for Christianity I may say so, a denial of Christ's teachings. Turkey broken down and torn with dissentions within may submit to the arrogant disposal of herself, and Indian Mahomedans may out of fear do likewise. Hindus out of fear, apathy or want of appreciation of the situation, may refuse to help their Mahomedan brethren in their hour of peril. The fact remains that a solemn promise of the Prime Minister of England has been wantonly broken. I will say nothing about President Wilson's fourteen points, for they seem now to be entirely forgotten as a day's wonder. It is a matter of deep sorrow that the Government of India

communique

offers a defence of the terms, calls them a fulfilment of Mr. Lloyd George's pledge of 5th January 1918 and yet apologises for their defective nature and appeals to the Mahomedans of India as if to mock them that they would accept the terms with quiet resignation. The mask that veils the hypocrisy is too thin to deceive anybody. It would have been dignified if the

communique

had boldly admitted Mr. Lloyd George's mistake in having made the promise referred to. As it is, the claim of fulfilment of the promise only adds to the irritation caused by its glaring breach. What is the use of the Viceroy saying, "The question of the Khilafat is one for the Mahomedans and Mahomedans only and that with their free choice in the matter Government have no desire to interfere," while the Khalif's dominions are ruthlessly dismembered, his control of the Holy places of Islam shamelessly taken away from him and he himself reduced to utter impotence in his own palace which can no longer be called a palace but which can he more fitly described us a prison? No wonder, His Excellency fears that the peace includes "terms which must be painful to all Moslems." Why should he insult Muslim intelligence by sending the Mussalmans of India a of encouragement and sympathy? Are they expected to find encouragement in the cruel recital of the arrogant terms or in a remembrance of 'the splendid response' made by them to the call of the King 'in the day of the Empire's need.' It ill becomes His Excellency to talk of the triumph of those ideals of justice and humanity for which the Allies fought. Indeed, the terms of the so called peace with Turkey if they are to last, will be a monument of human arrogance and man-made injustice. To attempt to crush the spirit of a brave and gallant race, because it has lost in the fortunes of war, is a triumph not of humanity but a demonstration of inhumanity. And if Turkey enjoyed the closest ties of friendship with Great Britain before the war, Great Britain has certainly made ample reparation for her mistake by having made the largest contribution to the humiliation of Turkey. It is insufferable therefore when the Viceroy feels confident that with the conclusion of this new treaty that friendship will quickly take life again and a Turkey regenerate full of hope and strength, will stand forth in the future as in the past a pillar of the Islamic faith. The Viceregal message audaciously concludes, "This thought will I trust strengthen you to accept the peace terms with resignation, courage and fortitude and to keep your loyalty towards the Crown bright and untarnished as it has been for so many generations." If Muslim loyalty remains untarnished it will certainly not be for want of effort on the part of the Government of India to put the heaviest strain upon it, but it will remain so because the Mahomedans realise their own strength--the strength in the knowledge that their cause is just and that they have got the power to vindicate justice in spite of the aberration suffered by Great Britain under a Prime Minister whom continued power has made as reckless in making promises as in breaking them.

Whilst therefore I admit that there is nothing either in the peace terms or in the Viceregal message covering them to inspire the Mahomedans and Indians in general with confidence or hope, I venture to suggest that there is no cause for despair and anger. Now is the time for Mahomedans to retain absolute self-control, to unite their forces and, weak though they are, with firm faith in God to carry on the struggle with redoubled vigour till justice is done. If India--both Hindu and Mahomedan--can act as one man and can withdraw her partnership in this crime against humanity which the peace terms represent, she will soon secure a revision of the treaty and give herself and the Empire at least, if not the world, a lasting peace. There is no doubt that the struggle would be bitter sharp and possibly prolonged, but it is worth all the sacrifice that it is likely to call forth. Both the Mussalmans and the Hindus are on their trial. Is the humiliation of the Khilafat a matter of concern to the former? And if it is, are they prepared to exercise restraint, religiously refrain from violence and practise non-co-operation without counting the material loss it may entail upon the community? Do the Hindus honestly feel for their Mahomedan brethren to the extent of sharing their sufferings to the fullest extent? The answer to these questions and not the peace terms, will finally decide the fate of the Khilafat.

MORE OBJECTIONS ANSWERED

Swadeshmitran

is one of the most influential Tamil dailies of Madras. It is widely read. Everything appearing in its columns is entitled to respect. The Editor has suggested some practical difficulty in the way of non-co-operation. I would therefore like, to the best of my ability, to deal with them.

I do not know where the information has been derived from that I have given up the last two stages of non-co-operation. What I have said is that they are a distant goal. I abide by it. I admit that all the stages are fraught with some danger, but the last two are fraught with the greatest--the last most of all. The stages have been fixed with a view to running the least possible risk. The last two stages will not be taken up unless the committee has attained sufficient control over the people to warrant the beliefs that the laying down of arms or suspension of taxes will, humanly speaking, be free from an outbreak of violence on the part of the people. I do entertain the belief that it is possible for the people to attain the discipline necessary for taking the two steps. When once they realise that violence is totally unnecessary to bend an unwilling government to their will and that the result can be obtained with certainty by dignified non-co-operation, they will cease to think of violence even by way of retaliation. The fact is that hitherto we have not attempted to take concerted and disciplined action from the masses. Some day, if we are to become truly a self-governing nation, that attempt has to be made. The present, in my opinion, is a propitious movement. Every Indian feels the insult to the Punjab as a personal wrong, every Mussalman resents the wrong done to the Khilafat. There is therefore a favourable atmosphere for expecting cohesive and restrained movement on the part of the masses.

So far as response is concerned, I agree with the Editor that the quickest and the largest response is to be expected in the matter of suspension of payment of taxes, but as I have said so long as the masses are not educated to appreciate the value of non-violence even whilst their holding are being sold, so long must it be difficult to take up the last stage into any appreciable extent.

I agree too that a sudden withdrawal of the military and the police will be a disaster if we have not acquired the ability to protect ourselves against robbers and thieves. But I suggest that when we are ready to call out the military and the police on an extensive scale we would find ourselves in a position to defend ourselves. If the police and the military resign from patriotic motives, I would certainly expect them to perform the same duty as national volunteers, not has hirelings but as willing protectors of the life and liberty of their countrymen. The movement of non-co-operation is one of automatic adjustment. If the Government schools are emptied, I would certainly expect national schools to come into being. If the lawyers as a whole suspended practice, they would devise arbitration courts and the nation will have expeditions and cheaper method of setting private disputes and awarding punishment to the wrong-doer. I may add that the Khilafat Committee is fully alive to the difficulty of the task and is taking all the necessary steps to meet the contingencies as they arise.

Regarding the leaving of civil employment, no danger is feared, because no one will leave his employment, unless he is in a position to find support for himself and family either through friends or otherwise.

Disapproval of the proposed withdrawal of students betrays, in my humble opinion, lack of appreciation of the true nature of non-co-operation. It is true enough that we pay the money wherewith our children are educated. But, when the agency imparting the education has become corrupt, we may not employ it without partaking of the agents, corruption. When students leave schools or colleges I hardly imagine that the teachers will fail to perceive the advisability of themselves resigning. But even if they do not, money can hardly be allowed to count where honour or religion are at the stake.

As to the boycott of the councils, it is not the entry of the Moderates or any other persons that matters so much as the entry of those who believe in non-co-operation. You may not co-operate at the top and non-co-operate at the bottom. A councillor cannot remain in the council and ask the *gumasta* who cleans the council-table to resign.

MR. PENNINGTON'S OBJECTIONS ANSWERED

I gladly publish Mr. Pennington's letter with its enclosure just as I have received them. Evidently Mr. Pennington is not a regular reader of 'Young India,' or he would have noticed that no one has condemned mob outrages more than I have. He seems to think that the article he has objected to was the only thing I have ever written on General Dyer. He does not seem to know that I have endeavoured with the utmost impartiality to examine the Jallianwala massacre. And he can see any day all the proof adduced by my fellow-commissioners and myself in support of our findings on the massacre. The ordinary readers of 'Young India' knew all the facts and therefore it was unnecessary for me to support my assertion otherwise. But unfortunately Mr. Pennington represents the typical Englishman. He does not want to be unjust, nevertheless he is rarely just in his appreciation of world events because he has no time to study them except cursorily and that through a press whose business is to air only party views. The average Englishman therefore except in parochial matters is perhaps the least informed though he claims to be well-informed about every variety of interest. Mr. Pennington's ignorance is thus typical of the others and affords the best reason for securing control of our own affairs in our own hands. Ability will come with use and not by waiting to be trained by those whose natural interest is to prolong the period of tutelage as much as possible.

But to return to Mr. Pennington's letter he complains that there has been no 'proper trial of any one.' The fault is not ours. India has consistently and insistently demanded a trial of all the officers concerned in the crimes against the Punjab.

He next objects to be 'violence' of my language. If truth is violent, I plead guilty to the charge of violence of language. But I could not, without doing violence to truth, refrain from using the language, I have, regarding General Dyer's action. It has been proved out of his own mouth or hostile witnesses:

(1) That the crowd was unarmed.

(2) That it contained children.

(3) That the 13th was the day of Vaisakhi fair.

(4) That thousands had come to the fair.

(5) That there was no rebellion.

(6) That during the intervening two days before the 'massacre' there was peace in Amritsar.

(7) That the proclamation of the meeting was made the same day as General Dyer's proclamation.

(8) That General Dyer's proclamation prohibited not meetings but processions or gatherings of four men on the streets and not in private or public places.

(9) That General Dyer ran no risk whether outside or inside the city.

(10) That he admitted himself that many in the crowd did not know anything of his proclamation.

(11) That he fired without warning the crowd and even after it had begun to disperse. He fired on the backs of the people who were in flight.

(12) That the men were practically penned in an enclosure.

In the face of these admitted facts I do call the deed a 'massacre.' The action amounted not to 'an error of judgment' but its 'paralysis in the face of fancied danger.'

I am sorry to have to say that Mr. Pennington's notes, which too the reader will find published elsewhere, betray as much ignorance as his letter.

Whatever was adopted on paper in the days of Canning was certainly not translated into action in its full sense. 'Promises made to the ear were broken to the hope,' was said by a reactionary Viceroy. Military expenditure has grown enormously since the days of Canning.

The demonstration in favour of General Dyer is practically a myth.

No trace was found of the so-called Danda Fauj dignified by the name of bludgeon-army by Mr. Pennington. There was no rebel army in Amritsar. The crown that committed the horrible murders and incendiarism contained no one community exclusively. The sheet was found posted only in Lahore and not in Amritsar. Mr. Pennington should moreover have known by this time that the meeting held on the 13th was held, among other things, for the purpose of condemning mob excesses. This was brought out at the Amritsar trial. Those who surrounded him could not stop General Dyer. He says he made up his mind to shoot in a moment. He consulted nobody. When the correspondent says that the troops would have objected to being concerned in 'what might in that case be not unfairly called a 'massacre,' he writes as if he had never lived in India. I wish the Indian troops had the moral courage to refuse to shoot innocent, unarmed men in full flight. But the Indian troops have been brought in too slavish an atmosphere to dare do any such correct act.

I hope Mr. Pennington will not accuse me again of making unverified assertions because I have not quoted from the books. The evidence is there for him to use. I can only assure him that the assertions are based on positive proofs mostly obtained from official sources.

Mr. Pennington wants me to publish an exact account of what happened on the 10th April. He can find it in the reports, and if he will patiently go through them he will discover that Sir Michael O'Dwyer and his officials goaded the people into frenzied fury--a fury which nobody, as I have already said, has condemned more than I have. The account of the following days is summed up in one word, *viz.* 'peace' on the part of the crowd disturbed by indiscriminate arrests, the massacre and the series of official crimes that followed.

I am prepared to give Mr. Pennington credit for seeking after the truth. But he has gone about it in the wrong manner. I suggest his reading the evidence before the Hunter Committee and the Congress Committee. He need not read the reports. But the evidence will convince him that I have understated the case against General Dyer.

When however I read his description of himself as "for 12 years Chief Magistrate of Districts in the South of India before reform, by assassination and otherwise, became so fashionable." I despair of his being able to find the truth. An angry or a biased man renders himself incapable of finding it. And Mr. Pennington is evidently both angry and biased. What does he mean by saying, "before reform by assassination and otherwise became so fashionable?" It ill becomes him to talk of assassination when the school of assassination seems happily to have become extinct. Englishmen will never see the truth so long as they permit their vision to be blinded by arrogant assumption of superiority or ignorant assumptions of infallibility.

MR. PENNINGTON'S LETTER TO MR. GANDHI

Dear Sir,

I do not like your scheme for "boycotting" the Government of India under what seems to be the somewhat less offensive (though more cumbrous) name of non-co-operation; but have always given you credit for a genuine desire to carry out revolution by peaceful means and am astonished at the violence of the language you use in describing General Dyer on page 4 of your issue of the 14th July last. You begin by saying that he is "by no means the worst offender," and, so far, I am inclined to agree, though as there has been no proper trial of anyone it is impossible to apportion their guilt; but then you say "his brutality is unmistakable," "his abject and unsoldierlike cowardice is apparent, he has called an *unarmed crowd* of men and children--mostly holiday makers--a rebel army." "He believes himself to be the saviour of the Punjab in that he was able to shoot down like rabbits men who were *penned* in an enclosure; such a man is unworthy to be considered a soldier. There was no bravery in his action. He ran no risk. He shot without the slightest opposition and without warning. This is not an error of judgement. It is paralysis of it in the face of *fancied* danger. It is proof of criminal incapacity and heartlessness," etc.

You must excuse me for saying that all this is mere rhetoric unsupported by any proof, even where proof was possible. To begin with, neither you nor I were present at the Jallianwalla

Bagh on that dreadful day--dreadful especially for General Dyer for whom you show no sympathy,--and therefore cannot know for certain whether the crowd was or was not unarmed.' That it was an 'illegal,' because a 'prohibited,' assembly is evident; for it is absurd to suppose that General Dyer's 4-1/2 hours march, through the city that very morning, during the whole of which he was warning the inhabitants against the danger of any sort of gathering, was not thoroughly well-known. You say they were 'mostly holiday makers,' but you give nor proof; and the idea of holiday gathering in Amritsar just then in incredible. I cannot understand your making such a suggestion. General Dyer was not the only officer present on the occasion and it is impossible to suppose that he would have been allowed to go on shooting into an innocent body of holiday-makers. Even the troops would have refused to carry out what might then have been not unfairly called a "massacre."

I notice that you never even allude to the frightful brutality of the mob which was immediately responsible for the punitive measure reluctantly adopted by General Dyer. Your sympathies seem to be only with the murderers, and I am not sanguine enough to suppose that my view of the case will have much influence with you. Still I am bound to do what I can to get at the truth, and enclose a copy of some notes I have had occasion to make. If you can publish an *exact* account of what happened at Amritsar on the 10th of April, 1919 and the following days, especially on the 13th, including the demonstration in favour of General Dyer, (if there was one), I for one, as a mere seeker after the truth, should be very much obliged to you. Mere abuse is not convincing, as you so often observe in your generally reasonable paper,

Yours faithfully, J. R. PENNINGTON, I.O.S. (Retd.) 35, VICTORIA ROAD, WORTHING, SUSSEX 27th Aug. 1920.

For 12 years Chief Magistrate of Districts in the south of India before reform, by assassination and otherwise, became so fashionable.

P.S. Let us get the case in this way. General Dyer, acting as the only representative of Government on the spot shot some hundreds of people (some of them *perhaps* innocently mixed up in an illegal assembly), in the *bona fide* belief that he was dealing with the remains of a very dangerous rebellion and was thereby saving the lives of very many thousands, and in the opinion of a great many people did actually save the city from falling in the hands of a dangerous mob.

SOME DOUBTS

Babu Janakdhari Prasad was a staunch coworker with me in Champaran. He has written a long letter setting forth his reasons for his belief that India has a great mission before her, and that she can achieve her purpose only by non-violent non-co-operation. But he has doubts which he would have me answer publicly. The letter being long, I am withholding. But the doubts are entitled to respect and I must endeavour to answer them. Here they are us framed by Bubu Janakdhari Prasad.

(a) Is not the non-co-operation movement creating a sort of race-hatred between Englishmen and Indians, and is it in accordance with the Divine plan of universal love and brotherhood?

(b) Does not the use of words "devilish," "satanic," etc., savour of unbrotherly sentiment and incite feelings of hatred?

(c) Should not the non-co-operation movement be conducted on strictly non-violent and non-emotional lines both in speech and action?

(d) Is there no danger of the movement going out of control and lending to violence?

As to (a), I must say that the movement is not 'creating' race-hatred. It certainly gives, as I have already said, disciplined expression to it. You cannot eradicate evil by ignoring it. It is because I want to promote universal brotherhood that I have taken up non-co-operation so that, by self-purification, India may make the world better than it is.

As to (b), I know that the words 'satanic' and 'devilish' are strong, but they relate the exact truth. They describe a system not persons: We are bound to hate evil, if we would shun it. But by means of non-co-operation we are able to distinguish between the evil and the evil-doer. I have found no difficulty in describing a particular activity of a brother of mine to be devilish, but I am not aware of having harboured any hatred about him. Non-co-operation teaches us to love our fellowmen in spite of their faults, not by ignoring or over-looking them.

As to (c), the movement is certainly being conducted on strictly non-violent lines. That all non-co-operators have not yet thoroughly imbibed the doctrine is true. But that just shows what an evil legacy we have inherited. Emotion there is in the movement. And it will remain. A man without emotion is a man without feeling.

As to (d), there certainly is danger of the movement becoming violent. But we may no more drop non-violent non-co-operation because of its dangers, than we may stop freedom because of the danger of its abuse.

REJOINDER

Messrs. Popley and Philips have been good enough to reply to my letter "To Every Englishman in India." I recognise and appreciate the friendly spirit of their letter. But I see that there are fundamental differences which must for the time being divide them and me. So long as I felt that, in spite of grievous lapses the British Empire represented an activity for the worlds and India's good, I clung to it like a child to its mother's breast. But that faith is gone. The British nation has endorsed the Punjab and Khilsfat crimes. The is no doubt a dissenting minority. But a dissenting minority that satisfies itself with a mere expression of its opinion and continues to help the wrong-doer partakes in wrong-doing.

And when the sum total of his energy represents a minus quantity one may not pick out the plus quantities, hold them up for admiration, and ask an admiring public to help regarding them. It is a favourite design of Satan to temper evil with a show of good and thus lure the unwary into the trap. The only way the world has known of defeating Satan is by shunning him. I invite Englishmen, who could work out the ideal the believe in, to join the ranks of the non-co-operationists. W.T. Stead prayed for the reverse of the British arms during the Boer war. Miss Hobbhouse invited the Boers to keep up the fight. The betrayal of India is much worse than the injustice done to the Boers. The Boers fought and bled for their rights. When therefore, we are prepared to bleed, the right will have become embodied, and idolatrous world will perceive it and do homage to it.

But Messers. Popley and Phillips object that I have allied myself with those who would draw the sword if they could. I see nothing wrong in it. They represent the right no less than I do. And is it not worth while trying to prevent an unsheathing of the sword by helping to win the bloodless battle? Those who recognise the truth of the Indian position can only do God's work by assisting this non-violent campaign.

The second objection raised by these English friends is more to the point. I would be guilty of wrong-doing myself if the Muslim cause was not just. The fact is that the Muslim claim is not to perpetuate foreign domination of non-Muslim or Turkish races. The Indian Mussalmans do not resist self-determination, but they would fight to the last the nefarious plan of exploiting Mesopotamia under the plea of self-determination. They must resist the studied attempt to humiliate Turkey and therefore Islam, under the false pretext of ensuring Armenian independence.

The third objection has reference to schools. I do object to missionary or any schools being carried on with Government money. It is true that it was at one time our money. Will these good missionaries be justified in educating me with funds given to them by a robber who has robbed me of my money, religion and honour because the money was originally mine.

I personally tolerated the financial robbery of India, but it would have been a sin to have tolerated the robbery of honour through the Punjab, and of religion through Turkey. This is strong language. But nothing less would truly describe my deep conviction. Needless to add that the emptying of Government aided, or affiliated, schools does not mean starving the young mind National Schools are coming into being as fast as the others are emptied.

Messrs. Popley and Phillips think that my sense of justice has been blurred by the knowledge of the Punjab and the Khilafat wrongs. I hope not. I have asked friends to show me some good fruit (intended and deliberately produced) of the British occupation of India. And I assure them that I shall make the amplest amends if I find that I have erred in my eagerness about the Khilafat and the Punjab wrongs.

TWO ENGLISHMEN REPLY

Dear Mr. Gandhi,

Thank you for your letter to every Englishman in India, with its hard-hitting and its generous tone. Something within us responds to the note which you have struck. We are not representatives of any corporate body, but we think that millions of our countrymen in England, and not a few in India, feel as we do. The reading of your letter convinces us that you and we cannot be real enemies.

May we say at once that in so far as the British Empire stands for the domination and exploitation of other races for Britain's benefit, for degrading treatment of any, for traffic in intoxicating liquors, for repressive legislation, for administration such as that which to the Amritsar incidents, we desire the end of it as much as you do? We quite understand that in the excitement of the present crisis, owing to certain acts of the British Administration, which we join with you in condemning, the Empire presents itself to you under this aspect along. But from personal contact with our countrymen, we know that working like leaven in the midst of such tendencies, as you and we deplore, is the faith in a better ideal--the ideal of a commonwealth of free peoples voluntarily linked together by the ties of common experience in the past and common aspirations for the future, a commonwealth which may hope to spread liberty and progress through the whole earth. With vast numbers of our countrymen we value the British Empire mainly as affording the possibility of the realization of such an idea and on the ground give it our loyal allegiance.

Meanwhile we do repent of that arrogant attitude to Indians which has been all too common among our countrymen, we do hold Indians to be our brothers and equals, many of them our superiors, and we would rather be servants than rulers of India. We desire an administration which cannot he intimated either by the selfish element in Anglo-Indian political opinion or by any other sectional interest and which shall govern in accordance with the best democratic principles. We should welcome the convening of a National assembly of recognized leaders of the people, representing all shades of political opinion of every caste, race and creed, to frame a constitution for Swaraj. In all the things that matter most we are with you. Surely you and we can co-operate in the service of India, in such matters for example as education. It seems to us nothing short of a tragedy that you should be rallying Indian Patriotism to inaugurate a new era of good will under a watchword that divides, instead of uniting all.

We have spoken of the large amount of common ground upon which you and we can stand. But frankness demands that we express our anxiety about some items in your programme. Leaving aside smaller questions on which your letter seems to us to do the British side less than justice, may we mention three main points? Your insistence on spiritual forces alone we deeply respect and desire to emulate, but we cannot understand your combining into it with a close alliance with those who, as you frankly say, would draw the sword as soon as they could.

Your desire for an education truly national commands our whole-hearted approval. But instead of Indianizing the present system, as you could begin to do from the beginning of next year, or instead of creating a hundred institutions such as that at Bolpur and turning into them the stream of India's young intellectual life, you appear to be turning that stream out of its present channel into open sands where it may dry up. In other words, you seem to us to be risking the complete cessation, for a period possibly, of years, of all education, for a large number of boys and young men. Is it best, for those young men or for India that the present imperfect education should cease before a better education is ready to take its place?

Your desire to unite Mohammedan and Hindu and to share with your Mohammedan brethren in seeking the satisfaction of Mohammedan aspirations, we can understand and sympathize with. But is there no danger, in the course which some of your party have urged upon the Government, that certain races in the former Ottoman Empire might be fixed under a foreign yoke, for worse than that which you hold the English yoke to be? You could not wish to purchase freedom in India at the price of enslavement in the middle East.

To sum up, we thank you for the spirit of your letter, to which we have tried to respond in the same spirit. We are with you in the desire for an India genuinely free to develop the best that is in her and in the belief that best is something wonderful of which the world to-day stands in need.

We are ready to co-operate with you and with every other man of any race or nationality who will help India to realize her best. Are you going to insist that you can have nothing to do with us if we receive a government grant (i.e., Indian money), for an Indian School. Surely some more inspiring battle cry than non-co-operation can be discovered. We have ventured quite frankly to point out three items in your present programme, which seem to us likely to hinder the attainment of your true ideals for Indian greatness. But those ideals themselves command our warm sympathy, and we desire to work, so far as we have opportunity, for their attainment. In fact, it is only thus that we can interpret our British citizenship.

Yours sincerely, (Sd.) H.A. POPLEY, (Sd.) G.E. PHILLIPS. Bangalore, November 15, 1920.

RENUNCIATION OF MEDALS

Mr. Gandhi has addressed the following letter to the Viceroy:--

It is not without a pang that I return the Kaisar-i-Hind gold medal granted to me by your predecessor for my humanitarian work in South Africa, the Zulu war medal granted in South Africa for my services as officer in charge of the Indian volunteer ambulance corps in 1906 and the Boer war medal fur my services as assistant superintendent of the Indian volunteer stretcher bearer corps during the Boer war of 1899-1900. I venture to return these medals in pursuance of the scheme of non-co-operation inaugurated to-day in connection with the Khilafat movement. Valuable as those honours have been to me, I cannot wear them with an easy conscience so long as my Mussalman countrymen have to labour under a wrong done to their religious sentiment. Events that have happened during the past month have confirmed me in the opinion that the Imperial Government have acted in the Khilafat matter in an unscrupulous, immoral and unjust manner and have been moving from wrong to wrong in order to defend their immorality. I can retain neither respect nor affection for such a Government.

The attitude of the Imperial and Your Excellency's Governments on the Punjab question has given me additional cause for grave dissatisfaction. I had the honour, as Your Excellency is aware, as one of the congress commissioners to investigate the causes of the disorders in the Punjab during the April of 1919. And it is my deliberate conviction that Sir Michael O'Dwyer was totally unfit to hold the office of Lieutenant Governor of Punjab and that his policy was primarily responsible for infuriating the mob at Amritsar. No doubt the mob excesses were unpardonable; incendiarism, murder of five innocent Englishmen and the cowardly assault on Miss Sherwood were most deplorable and uncalled for. But the punitive measures taken by General Dyer, Col. Frank Johnson, Col. O'Brien, Mr. Bosworth Smith, Rai Shri Ram Sud, Mr. Malik Khan and other officers were out of all proportional to the crime of the people and amounted to wanton cruelty and inhumanity and almost unparalleled in modern times. Your excellency's light-hearted treatment of the official crime, your, exoneration of Sir Michael O'Dwyer, Mr. Montagu's dispatch and above all the shameful ignorance of the Punjab events and callous disregard of the feelings of Indians betrayed by the House of Lords, have filled me with the gravest misgivings regarding the future of the Empire, have estranged me completely from the present Government and have disabled me from tendering, as I have hitherto whole-heartedly tendered, my loyal co-operation.

In my humble opinion the ordinary method of agitating by way of petitions, deputations and the like is no remedy for moving to repentence a Government so hopelessly indifferent to the welfare of its charges as the Government of India has proved to me. In European countries, condonation of such grievous wrongs as the Khilafat and the Punjab would have resulted in a bloody revolution by the people. They would have resisted at all costs national emasculation such as the said wrongs imply. But half of India is to weak to offer violent resistance and the other half is unwilling to do so.

I have therefore ventured to suggest the remedy of non-co-operation which enables those who wish, to dissociate themselves from the Government and which, if it is unattended by violence and undertaken in an ordered manner, must compel it to retrace its steps and undo the wrongs committed. But whilst I shall pursue the policy of non-co-operation in so far as I can carry the people with me, I shall not lose hope that you will yet see your way to do justice. I therefore respectfully ask Your Excellency to summon a conference of the recognised leaders of the people and in consultation with them find a way that would placate the Mussalmans and do reparation to the unhappy Punjab. *August 4, 1920.*

MAHATMA GANDHI'S LETTER TO H.R.H. THE DUKE OF CON-NAUGHT

The following letter has been addressed by Mr. Gandhi to his Royal Highness the Duke of Connaught;--

Sir,

Your Royal Highness must have heard a great deal about non-co-operation, non-co-operationists and their methods and incidentally of me its humble author. I fear that the information given to Your Royal Highness must have been in its nature one-sided. I owe it to you and to my friends and myself that I should place before you what I conceive to be the scope of non-co-operation as followed not only be me but my closest associates such as Messrs. Shaukat Ali and Mahomed Ali.

For me it is no joy and pleasure to be actively associated in the boycott of your Royal Highness' visit--I have tendered loyal and voluntary association to the Government for an unbroken period of nearly 30 years in the full belief that through that way lay the path of freedom for my country. It was therefore no slight thing for me to suggest to my countrymen that we should take no part in welcoming Your Royal Highness. Not one among us has anything against you as an English gentleman. We hold your person as sacred as that of a dearest friend. I do not know any of my friends who would not guard it with his life, if he found it in danger. We are not at war with individual Englishmen we seek not to destroy English life. We do desire to destroy a system that has emasculated our country in body, mind and soul. We are determined to battle with all our might against that in the English nature which has made O'Dwyerism and Dyerism possible in the Punjab and has resulted in a wanton affront upon Islam a faith professed by seven crores of our countrymen. The affront has been put in breach of the letter and the spirit of the solemn declaration of the Prime Minister. We consider it to be inconsistent with our self respect any longer to brook the spirit of superiority and dominance which has systematically ignored and disregarded the sentiments of thirty crores of the innocent people of India on many a vital matter. It is humiliating to us, it cannot be a matter of pride to you, that thirty crores of Indians should live day in and day out in the fear of their lives from one hundred thousand Englishmen and therefore be under subjection to them.

Your Royal Highness has come not to end the system I have described but to sustain it by upholding its prestige. Your first pronouncement was a laudation of Lord Wellingdon. I have the privilege of knowing him. I believe him to be an honest and amiable gentleman who will not willingly hurt even a fly. But, he has certainly failed as a ruler. He allowed himself to be guided by those whose interest it was to support their power. He is reading the mind of the Dravidian province. Here in Bengal you are issuing a certificate of merit to a Governor who is again from all I have heard an estimable gentleman. But he knows nothing of the heart of Bengal and its yearnings. Bengal is not Calcutta. Fort William and the palaces of Calcutta represent an insolent exploitation of the unmurmuring and highly cultured peasantry of this fair province. Non-co-operationists have come to the conclusion that they must not be deceived by the reforms that tinker with the problem of India's distress and humiliation. Nor must they be impatient and angry. We must not in our impatient anger resort, to stupid violence. We freely admit that we must take our due share of the blame for the existing state. It is not so much the British guns that are responsible fur our subjection, as our voluntary co-operation. Our non-participation in a hearty welcome to your Royal Highness is thus in no sense a demonstration against your high personage but it is against the system you have come to uphold. I know that individual Englishmen cannot even if they will alter the English nature all of a sudden. If we would be equals of Englishmen we must cast off fear. We must learn to be self-reliant and independent of the schools, courts, protection, and patronage of a Government, we seek to end, if it will not mend. Hence this non-violent non-co-operation. I know that we have not all yet become non-violent in speech and deed. But the results so far achieved have I assure Your Royal Highness, been amazing. The people have understood the secret and the value of non-violence as they have never done before. He who runs may see that this a religious, purifying movement. We are leaving off drink, we are trying to rid India of the curse of untouchability. We are trying to throw off foreign tinsel splendour and by reverting to the spinning wheel reviving the ancient and the poetic simplicity of life. We hope thereby to sterilize the existing harmful institution. I ask Your Royal Highness as an Englishman to study this movement and its possibilities for the Empire and the world. We are at war with nothing that is good in the world. In protecting Islam in the manner we are, we are protecting all religions. In protecting the honour of India we are protecting the honour of humanity. For our means are hurtful to none. We desire to live on terms of friendship with Englishmen but that friendship must be friendship of equals in both theory and practice. And we must continue to non-co-operate, i.e. to purify ourselves till the goal is achieved.

I ask Your Royal Highness and through you every Englishman to appreciate the view-point of the non-co-operationists.

I beg to remain, Your Royal Highness's faithful servant, (Sd.) M.K. GANDHI. *February*, 1921

THE GREATEST THING

It is to be wished that non-co-operationists will clearly recognise that nothing can stop the onward march of the nation as violence. Ireland may gain its freedom by violence. Turkey may regain her lost possessions by violence within measurable distance of time. But India cannot win her freedom by violence for a century, because her people are not built in the manner of other nations. They have been nurtured in the traditions of suffering. Rightly or wrongly, for good or ill, Islam too has evolved along peaceful lines in India. And I make bold to say that, if the honour of Islam is to be vindicated through its followers in India, it will only be by methods of peaceful, silent, dignified, conscious, and courageous suffering. The more I study that wonderful faith, the more convinced I become that the glory of Islam is due not to the sword but to the sufferings, the renunciation, and the nobility of its early Caliphs. Islam decayed when its followers, mistaking the evil for the good, dangled the sword in the face of man, and lost sight of the godliness, the humility, and austerity of its founder and his disciples. But, I am not at the present moment, concerned with showing that the basis of Islam, as of all religions, is not violence but suffering not the taking of life but the giving of it.

What I am anxious to show is that non-co-operationists must be true as well to the spirit as to the letter of their vow if they would gain Swaraj within one year. They may forget non-co-operation but they dare not forget non-violence. Indeed, non-co-operation is non-violence. We are violent when we sustain a government whose creed is violence. It bases itself finally not on right but on might. Its last appeal is not to reason, nor the heart, but to the sword. We are tired of this creed and we have risen against it. Let us not ourselves belie our profession by being violent. Though the English are very few, they are organised for violence. Though we are many we cannot be organised for violence for a long time to come. Violence for us is a gospel or despair.

I have seen a pathetic letter from a god-fearing English woman who defends Dyerism for she thinks that, if General Dyer had not enacted Jallianwala, women and children would have been murdered by us. If we are such brutes as to desire the blood of innocent women and children, we deserve to be blotted out from the face of the earth. There is the other side. It did not strike this good lady that, if we were friends, the price that her countrymen paid at Jallianwala for buying their safety was too great. They gained their safety at the cost of their humanity. General Dyer has been haltingly blamed, and his evil genius Sir Michael O'Dwyer entirely exonerated because Englishmen do not want to leave this country of fields even if everyone of us has to be killed. If we go mad again as we did at Amritsar, let there be no mistake that a blacker Jallianwala will be enacted.

Shall we copy Dyerism and O'Dwyerism even whilst we are condemning it? Let not our rock be violence and devilry. Our rock must be non-violence and godliness. Let us, workers, be clear as to what we are about. *Swaraj depends upon our ability to control all the forces of violence on our side.* Therefore there is no Swaraj within one year, if there is violence on the part of the people.

We must then refrain from sitting *dhurna*, we must refrain from crying 'shame, shame' to anybody, we must not use any coercion to persuade our people to adopt our way. We must guarantee to them the same freedom we claim for ourselves. We must not tamper with the masses. It is dangerous to make political use of factory labourers or the peasantry--not that we are not entitled to do so, but we are not ready for it. We have neglected their political (as distinguished from literary) education all these long years. We have not got enough honest, intelligent, reliable, and brave workers to enable us to act upon these countrymen of ours.

IX-MAHATMA GANDHI'S STATEMENT

[The following is the Statement of Mahatma Gandhi made before the Court during his Trial in Ahmedabad on the 18th March 1921.]

Before reading his written statement Mahatma Gandhi spoke a few words as introductory remarks to the whole statement. He said: Before I read this statement, I would like to state that I entirely endorse the learned Advocate-General's remarks in connection with my humble self. I think that he was entirely fair to me in all the statements that he has made, because it is very true and I have no desire whatsoever to conceal from this Court the fact that to preach disaffection towards the existing system of Government has become almost a passion with me. And the learned Advocate-General is also entirely in the right when he says that my preaching of disaffection did not commence with my connection with "Young India" but that it commenced much earlier and in the statement that I am about to read it will be my painful duty to admit before this Court that it commenced much earlier than the period stated by the Advocate-General. It is the most painful duty with me but I have to discharge that duty knowing the responsibility that rested upon my shoulders. And I wish to endorse all the blame that the Advocate-General has thrown on my shoulders in connection with the Bombay occurrence, Madras occurrences, and the Chouri Choura occurrences thinking over these things deeply, and sleeping over them night after night and examining my heart I have come to the conclusion that it is impossible for me to dissociate myself from the diabolical crimes of Chouri Choura or the mad outrages of Bombay. He is quite right when he says that as a man of responsibility, a man having received a fair share of education, having had a fair share of experience of this world, I should know them. I knew that I was playing with fire. I ran the risk and if I was set free I would still do the same. I would be failing in my duty if I do not do so. I have felt it this morning that I would have failed in my duty if I did not say all what I said here just now. I wanted to avoid violence. Non-violence is the first article of my faith. It is the last article of my faith. But I had to make my choice. I had either to submit to a system which I considered has done an irreparable harm to my country or incur the risk of the mad fury of my people bursting forth when they understood the truth from my lips. I know that my people have sometimes gone mad. I am deeply sorry for it; and I am, therefore, here to submit not to a light penalty but to the highest penalty. I do not ask for mercy. I do not plead any extenuating act. I am here, therefore, to invite and submit to the highest penalty that can be inflicted upon me for what in law is a deliberate crime and what appears to me to be the highest duty of a citizen. The only course open to you, Mr. Judge, is, as I am just going to say in my statement, either to resign your post or inflict on me the severest penalty if you believe that the system and law you are assisting to administer are good for the people. I do not expect that kind of conversion. But by the time I have finished with my statement you will, perhaps, have a glimpse of what is raging within my breast to run this maddest risk which a sane man can run.

WRITTEN STATEMENT

I owe it perhaps to the Indian public and to the public in England to placate which this prosecution is mainly taken up that I should explain why from a staunch loyalist and co-operator I have become an uncompromising disaffectionist and non-co-operator. To the Court too I should say why I plead guilty to the charge of promoting disaffection towards the Government established by law in India. My public life began in 1893 in South Africa in troubled weather. My first contact with British authority in that country was not of a happy character. I discovered that as a man and as an Indian I had no rights. On the contrary I discovered that I had no rights as a man because I was an Indian.

But I was not baffled. I thought that this treatment of Indians was an excrescence upon a system that was intrinsically and mainly good. I gave the Government my voluntary and hearty co-operation, criticising it fully where I felt it was faulty but never wishing its destruction.

Consequently when the existence of the Empire was threatened in 1899 by the Boer challenge, I offered my services to it, raised a volunteer ambulance corps and served at several actions that took place for the relief of Ladysmith. Similarly in 1906 at the time of the Zulu revolt I raised a stretcher-bearer party and served till the end of the 'rebellion'. On both these occasions I received medals and was even mentioned in despatches. For my work in South Africa I was given by Lord Hardinge a Kaiser-i-Hind Gold Medal. When the war broke out in 1914 between England and Germany I raised a volunteer ambulance corps in London consisting of the then resident Indians in London, chiefly students. Its work was acknowledged by the authorities to be valuable. Lastly in India when a special appeal was made at the War Conference in Delhi in 1917 by Lord Chelmsford for recruits, I struggled at the cost of my health to raise a corps in Kheda and the response was being made when the hostilities ceased and orders were received that no more recruits were wanted. In all those efforts at service I was actuated by the belief that it was possible by such services to gain a status of full equality in the Empire for my countrymen.

The first shock came in the shape of the Rowlalt Act a law designed to rob the people of all real freedom. I felt called upon to lead an intensive agitation against it. Then followed the Punjab horrors beginning with the massacre at Jallianwala Bagh and culminating in brawling orders, public floggings and other indescribable humiliations, I discovered too that the plighted word of the Prime Minister to the Mussalmans of India regarding the integrity of Turkey and the holy places of Islam was not likely to be fulfilled. But in spite of the foreboding and the grave warnings of friends, at the Amritsar Congress in 1919 I fought for co-operation and working the Montagu-Chelmsford reforms, hoping that the Prime Minister would redeem his promise to the Indian Mussalmans, that the Punjab wound would be healed and that the reforms inadequate and unsatisfactory though they were, marked a new era of hope in the life of India. But all that hope was shattered. The Khilafat promise was not to be redeemed. The Punjab crime was white-washed and most culprits went not only unpunished but remained in service and some continued to draw pensions from the Indian revenue, and in some cases were even rewarded. I saw too that not only did the reforms not mark a change of heart, but they were only a method of further draining India of her wealth and of prolonging her servitude.

I came reluctantly to the conclusion that the British connection had made India more helpless than she ever was before, politically and economically. A disarmed India has no power of resistance against any aggressor if she wanted to engage in an armed conflict with him. So much is this the case that some of our best men consider that India must take generations before she can achieve the Dominion status. She has become so poor that she has little power of resisting famines. Before the British advent India spun and wove in her millions of cottages just the supplement she needed for adding to her meagre agricultural resources. The cottage industry, so vital for India's existence, has been ruined by incredibly heartless and inhuman processes as described by English witnesses. Little do town-dwellers know how the semi-starved masses of Indians are slowly sinking to lifelessness. Little do they know that their miserable comfort represents the brokerage they get for the work they do for the foreign exploiter, that the profits and the brokerage are sucked from the masses. Little do they realise that the Government established by law in British India is carried on for this exploitation of the masses. No sophistry, no jugglery in figures can explain away the evidence the skeletons in many villages present to the naked eye. I have no doubt whatsoever that both England and the town dwellers of India will have to answer, if there is a God above, for this crime against humanity which is perhaps unequalled in history. The law itself in this country has been used to serve the foreign exploiter. My unbiased, examination of the Punjab Martial Law cases had led me to believe that at least ninety-five per cent. of convictions were wholly bad. My experience of political cases in India leads me to the conclusion that in nine out of every ten the condemned men were totally innocent. Their crime consisted in love of their country. In ninety-nine cases out of hundred justice has been denied to Indians as against Europeans in the Court of India. This is not an exaggerated picture. It is the experience of almost every Indian who has had anything to do such cases. In my opinion the administration of the law is thus prostituted consciously or unconsciously for the benefit of the exploiter. The greatest misfortune is that Englishmen and their Indian associates in the administration of the country do not know that they are engaged in the crime I have attempted to describe. I am satisfied that many English and Indian officials honestly believe that they are administering one of the best systems devised in the world and that India is making steady though slow progress. They do not know that a subtle but effective system of terrorism and an organised display of force on the one hand and the deprivation of all powers of retaliation of self-defence on the other have emasculated the people and induced in them the habit of simulation. This awful habit has added to the ignorance and the self-deception of the administrators. Section 124-A under which I am happily charged is perhaps the prince among the political sections of the Indian Penal Code designed to suppress the liberty of the citizen. Affection cannot be manufactured or regulated by law. If one has no affection for a person or thing one should be free to give the fullest expression to his disaffection so long as he does not contemplate, promote or incite to violence. But the section under which mere promotion of disaffection is a crime. I have studied some of the cases tried under it, and I know that some of the most loved of India's patriots have been convicted under it. I consider it a privilege therefore, to be charged under it. I have endeavoured to give in their briefest outline the reasons for my disaffection. I have no personal ill-will against any single administrator, much less can I have any disaffection towards the King's person. But I hold it to be a virtue to be disaffected towards a Government which in its totality has done more harm to India than any previous system. India is less manly under the British rule than she ever was before. Holding such a belief, I consider it to be a sin to have affection for the system. And it has been a precious privilege for me to be able to write what I have in the various articles tendered in evidence against me.

In fact I believe that I have rendered a service to India and England by showing in non-co-operation the way out of the unnatural state in which both are living. In my humble opinion, non-co-operation with evil is as much a duty as is co-operation with good. But in the past, non-co-operation has been deliberately expressed in violence to the evil doer. I am endeavouring to show to my countrymen that violent non-co-operation only multiplies evil and that as evil can only be sustained by violence, withdrawal of support of evil requires complete abstention from violence. Non-violent implies voluntary submission to the penalty for non-co-operation with evil. I am here, therefore, to invite and submit cheerfully to the highest penalty that can he inflicted upon me for what in law is a deliberate crime and what appears to me to be the highest duty of a citizen. The only course open to you, the Judge and the Assessors, is either to resign your posts and thus dissociate yourselves from evil if you feel that the law you are called upon to administer is an evil and that in reality I am innocent, or to inflict on me the severest penalty if you believe that the system and the law you are assisting to administer are good for the people of this country and that my activity is therefore injurious to the public weal.

M. K. GHANDI.